MAGIC AND RHETORIC IN ANCIENT GREECE

The Carl Newell Jackson Lectures, 1974

Magic and Rhetoric
in Ancient Greece

Jacqueline de Romilly

Harvard University Press
Cambridge, Massachusetts
and London, England
1975

Acknowledgments

This book consists of the four Carl Newell Jackson Lectures that I had the honor of delivering at Harvard University in April 1974, and it should begin with a word of gratitude to the eminent founder of these lectures.

But it would be most unfair not to thank also the members of the Department of the Classics, and Professor Glen Bowersock, the chairman of this department: I cannot forget the extreme kindness that I experienced every day and that made this occasion exceptionally delightful to me. Several professors and students helped me with their remarks. It is a pleasure for me to recall the fact that Professor Emily Vermeule called my attention to a small detail, which indeed could be the justification of my theme—namely, that *glamour* and *grammar* or, in French, *grimoire* and *grammaire* were originally the same word and thus combined, even in the vocabulary, the magical and rationalistic aspects of speech. To Anne Whitman also, who corrected my manuscript with so much insight and generosity, I feel deeply and sincerely grateful.

Jacqueline de Romilly

Contents

I

Gorgias and Magic

I I am not at all sure I am the right person to deal with the theme I have chosen for this series of lectures; in fact, I doubt it very much. But I am sure the problem of the relationship between magic and rhetoric in ancient Greece exists and has a meaning. It was not suggested to me by modern discussions about language and literature; rather, it has a precise starting point a long way in the past—namely, in Gorgias, the sophist of the fifth century B.C. Gorgias, in the *Helen*, insists on the wonderful power of speech, and he does so by using two similes comparing speech with poetry on the one hand and magic on the other.

Helen, he says, could not resist the power of *logos*, for it is a great power; and he remarks, in §9, that speech is close to poetry: "Poetry I consider and call speech with rhythm; now those who hear it are seized by shuddering fright and weeping pity and sorrowful longing." He even comments on the fact that the soul should be thus personally affected by what happens to other people.[1] Then he starts a fresh argument and says (§10): "The divine charms working through words can bring both pleasure and pain"; and in a luxurious bunch of words he combines all the expressions that can be used for magic and witchcraft: ἔθελξε, γοητεία, γοητείας καὶ μαγείας, to which will be added, in §14, ἐφαρμάκευσαν καὶ ἐξεγοήτευσαν. The spell of words is firmly assimilated to witchcraft. This very insistence shows that what we have here is more than a mere simile; in fact, the double analogy drawn by Gorgias may well turn out to be a program for rhetoric.

I am not going to describe the psychology on which such an idea of the power of speech may rest; this has been done by Charles Segal.[2] I shall keep quite close to our double analogy; and my problem will here be to see what range and influence it had on the origin and establishment of rhetoric as such.

But first I must bring in another word of justification. I have announced a double analogy; why, after having focused my theme on magic, do I drag in poetry as well? The reason is quite simple. The influence of poetry, as Gorgias describes it, is already of a magical nature.

Indeed, poetry at first was something divine. There even existed a number of poets who were superhuman creatures and whose powers, in all sorts of matters, were both mysterious and great. Orpheus and Empedocles were endowed with such powers. As for ordinary poets, they were believed to receive their inspiration from the Muses, and the miraculous action of these divine beings was thus transferred to their poems. I have tried to show in a recent paper how, from Homer to Hesiod and Pindar, this magical influence came to be more and more directly attributed to the poet.[3] Also, the action of these poems on the feelings of the audience was more and more emphasized. In Homer, only the Sirens seem to cast a spell.[4] In Hesiod, one hears about forgetting all sorrows (*Theogony* 102). In Pindar, music acts as a magic charm and lulls away all anger in the beginning of *Pythian* 1, where we find the word θέλγειν and the notion of being possessed by something cast upon you: ῥιπαῖσι κατασχόμενος. We also hear that poets can brush away fatigue, or persuade people, as with a φίλτρον, a spell.[5]

This is indeed a magical action, and one that could explain the principle underlying Gorgias' description of poetry. Yet it leaves us far from the varied emotions stirred by poetry according to him. What has happened in between? What, if not tragedy and its lies?

That poets could lie had also been discovered progressively, from Homer to Hesiod, Parmenides, Solon, and

Pindar. But their deceptions were viewed as only disquieting accidents. Tragedy, on the other hand, rested on impersonation, a fact that of course puzzled some sophists and philosophers, who were trying to figure out the relation of true and untrue, real or unreal. Among them was Gorgias, and we know that he used to say tragedy was by nature deceit, ἀπάτη.[6] Much has been written on this notion of ἀπάτη, but we shall not go into it at present. I shall only call attention to the fact that, in the passage of the *Helen* dealing with *logos*, the verb ἀπατᾶσθαι comes in twice; for one of the powers of speech is deception, which it achieves thanks to the shortcomings of human judgment. Rhetoric and tragedy have at least this in common.

They have much more, if we consider what they aim at—namely, stirring varied emotions.

Before the existence of tragedy, poets pretended only to be able to create the magic peace and pleasure connected with inspired music. After the development of tragedy, Gorgias could add to these unemotional feelings the two specifically tragic emotions of fear and pity ("shuddering fright and weeping pity"); and he insisted on the possibility of thus creating a personal reaction to the good or bad fortune of other people, which was to remain characteristic of tragedy.[7] It is almost too obvious to point out that Aristotle's description is exactly the same, and that these two emotions are exactly those he mentions as the aim and result of tragedy. It might seem more surprising to find in Gorgias a third emotion, which was not to acquire such great fame: he adds "sorrowful longing," πόθος φιλοπενθής. Why? The word πόθος could, no doubt, have been chosen as suggesting love and applying to Helen's case, with which Gorgias is dealing. But φιλοπενθής goes much beyond that particular case, and it is difficult not to connect it with the occasions on which Homer's poetry made people weep, or wish to weep: ἵμερον ὦρσε γόοιο. This happens when he reminds people of the dead or the absent and thus inspires them with πόθος.[8] Gorgias' πόθος φιλοπενθὴς is thus a sort of inheritance from the epic. Yet it could also be argued that, even if the expression does not apply to the actual emotions stirred by tragedy, it does apply to the enjoyment of sorrow and of tears, which is the paradox of tragedy as a whole.[9]

Rhetoric, then, could find a model in the influence of poetry, particularly tragic poetry. And the masters of rhetoric, who wanted to claim this power for themselves, had only to try and classify these emotions and eventually add some new ones, which the practical use of speech could suggest or require. Now this is exactly what took place, both in Gorgias' text and in other authors after him.

Even before poetry is mentioned, Gorgias says that speech can stop fear and banish sorrow, inspire joy and develop pity; pity and fear reappear when he speaks of poetry, but sorrow and joy do not, perhaps because these two emotions suggest a more direct reference to one's own situation.[10] And toward the end of the text, after the passage on poetry, we again find something slightly different: speech, says Gorgias, can produce sorrow and pleasure, fright or confidence (14). This is almost the same set of emotions, but not quite, for we find here a desire to be more systematical; fright and confidence form a pair of complementary emotions, as do pleasure and pain. The theory seems to get really into shape.

Similarly, we know from Plato and his commentators[11] that Thrasymachus was famous for the way in which he could produce sorrow in the audience (or, as Hermias says, pity), or anger, or soothe these emotions, as by magic (ἐπᾴδων). This he did by ready-made topics, specially worked up for that purpose. The same notion about the power of speech recurs in Sophocles' last play, where it is said that words can move people, by producing pleasure, displeasure, or pity (*Oedipus Coloneus* 1281–1282), or can indeed cast away anger, as by some sort of incantation (1194).

If we trace the idea as far as Aristotle's *Rhetoric*, what we find is again a list of emotions, or πάθη. This list is now much longer, for Aristotle treats not only anger and calm (like Thrasymachus), fear and confidence (like Gorgias), pity (like both of them), but also indignation, friendship and hatred, shame and impudence, readiness to oblige and its contrary, envy and emulation.[12] But whatever the list and the number of antagonistic emotions it contains, it is obvious that the very aim of rhetoric was thus fixed at the start by Gorgias' reference to the irrational influence of poetry, and particularly of tragic poetry.

It should be added that, by a sort of reciprocal influence, poetry was more and more treated as a kind of proto-rhetoric.[13] Plato described, for instance, the manner in which the rhapsode produces fear and sorrow (*Ion* 535c–d). He also imagined a man who thought he was a tragic poet, only because he was able to write, about any subject, either very long or very short developments (ῥήσεις) that could stir pity or fear in the audience (*Phaedrus* 268c). Tragedy Plato treated as a kind of flattery, like rhetoric (*Gorgias* 502b). Indeed, by a nice shifting of what Gorgias had said in the *Helen*, he declared that if one took away from poetry the rhythm and meter, there just remained speech, *logoi* (502c). Later still, Aristotle was to call Homer the master of lies and fake reasoning (*Poetics* 1460.17 ff). The assimilation of rhetoric to poetry altered the very view that people had of poetry.

But, remarkable as such an assimilation may be as regards the aims of poetry and rhetoric, it does not stop there; for the master of rhetoric could also find in the poets some notion about the means by which this aim could be reached. One of these means is suggested in Gorgias' text—namely, style.

When Gorgias declares that poetry is only speech with rhythm, some people think he is gravely misunderstanding the nature of poetry. I am not sure that is right; it would be more exact to say that he had an exceptionally high idea of the possibilities of prose, which he raises to the level of poetry.

We do not know enough about dates or doctrines to be able to link precisely the invention of poetic style in prose to anyone in particular among the sophists. But the general tendency is clear. All the sophists and thinkers of the late fifth century were interested in the means and nature of such a style. Protagoras used to lecture on poets, Hippias on rhythm and meters. Democritus also wrote on rhythm and harmony. All this surely helped in launching poetical prose and the elevated style that Gorgias was to represent for later theorists.

Poetical prose [14] was invented in order to emulate, and imitate, the dignity of poetry. Isocrates, who wrote a very pure prose without any of the strange effects used by Gorgias, but who had been a disciple of his,[15] always remained conscious of the challenge offered by poetry. In the *Evagoras* (10–11) he regrets that orators cannot use the rare words and rhythm that are the privilege of poetry and that, by the sole action of harmony, move the audience into a kind of rapture (ψυχαγωγοῦσιν). Yet he accepts the challenge, for he has a high idea of literary prose. In the *Antidosis* he is even proud to develop a long analysis stressing that "some people" (like himself and Gorgias) do not write on petty matters but on general themes of interest to all Greece and thus compose speeches that are "more similar to those made with music and rhythm than to those delivered in the courts of justice." These speeches, he says, "have a more poetical and more brilliant style (47: ποιητικώτερα καὶ ποικιλώτερα), more noble ideas, more dignified themes" than the others. Therefore they are heard with as much eagerness as "those in poetry" (τῶν ἐν τοῖς μέτροις πεποιημένων). Literary prose was thus created with a view to emulating poetry[16]—which is exactly the view put forward in Gorgias' text. This accounts for some of the features characteristic of literary prose in ancient Greece.

First, rhythm. Both Gorgias and Thrasymachus were known to have cultivated in prose some of the rules of poetry. Thrasymachus was an adept in rhythm and is mentioned by Aristotle as having had a predilection for the paeon (*Rhetoric* 3.8, 1409a2).[17] Both Thrasymachus and Gorgias started avoiding hiatus, as was the rule in poetry,[18] and Isocrates was to turn that habit into a real rule of Greek prose.

But we have more than rhythm. Though I shall not here go into the question of Gorgian figures of style, which will be dealt with later, one of them at least suggests a connection with poetry—namely, the use of antithesis.[19] Indeed, among the means by which poetry could work upon people's emotions, antithesis had its place, since it enhanced the meaning and made it more powerful. All tragedies use it. Now, I do not need to dwell upon this theme at John Finley's university, as he has made such a good point in his study "The Origins of Thucydides' Style,"[20] where he traces antithetical style in Sophocles and Euripides and shows it to have been a feature of the Periclean Age. He explains its success as due to sophistic influences current in Thucydides' youth and apparent in tragedy before 427. The tragedies of that period, such as the *Antigone*, *Medea*, and *Ajax*, were particularly rich in such figures.

It seems certain that Gorgias did not invent antithesis, which had long been familiar in Greek poetry; the examples collected by Karl Reich, as early as 1909, are indeed eloquent.[21] I am also ready to believe that Gorgias was not the first to use it in prose; this seems likely enough even if one does not share John Finley's opinion about the date of Antiphon's works. Yet two facts remain, which are the only important ones for our theme. One, that antithesis was first used in poetry; even if prose writers and orators contributed to its diffusion in contemporary tragedy, they had first found it used by poets. And, although Gorgias did not launch the fashion, it can be admitted that such a style would not have been so repeatedly ascribed to him if our sophist had not turned this feature into a theory, or at least into a systematic habit, or if he had not insisted, with particular emphasis, on style in general. Protagoras, Thrasymachus, and others certainly worked along the same line.[22] But they were interested mainly in arguments, whereas Gorgias relished style. As a matter of fact, when Aristotle mentions this borrowing of poetic style from poetry and declares that the glamour of poetry led, at first, to the creation of poetic diction, he does not say this diction started "in Gorgias"; he just gives Gorgias as the most telling example and writes "as we see in Gorgias" (*Rhetoric* 3.1, 1404a26: οἷον ἡ Γοργίου)—that is to say, Gorgias practiced it more conspicuously than anybody else.

The same notion would also avail for other features of poetic style, such as the use of rare and poetical words, which can add majesty to the style. Even Aristotle admits it (*Rhetoric* 3.2, 1404b5 ff). Now, he does not actually mention Gorgias in this context; but, also in book 3, he quotes Gorgias among three authors who exaggerated the habit of using compound words (1405b37), and cites him again, with only one other author, for his exaggerated and obscure metaphors, adding to his quotations that this was too much like poets' habits: ποιητικῶς γὰρ ἄγαν (1406b10).[23]

But perhaps the obvious link thus established by Gorgias between poetry and rhetoric—a link concerning both their aims and their means—would not have been so much insisted upon, since it was a common feature of literary style, if there had not been another, more specific connection, appearing in his teaching and in his style: precisely the connection with magic itself.

When dealing with the power of poetry, we saw that this power was in fact considered as magic. It was irrational, it came from the gods, it was a charm (θελκτήριον). Now that we come to magic proper, we must first observe that it is directly connected with poetry. We have a number of magic formulas, generally written on tablets, which were then buried, or eventually written on papyri. But this is the lowest and latest level of magic spells. What we know of magic rests mainly on the poets.

If we consider the earliest times, the difference between religion and magic is not easy to draw. It may be difficult to trace at any time,[24] but, given the piety of ancient times, the difficulty is even greater. A seer can tell the future; thanks to the gods, he is, in a way, a fortuneteller. An offering to the nether gods can call up a dead man from among the dead—whether he appears in full sight as a phantom or manifests his presence by a mysterious action and ghostly intervention; that is to say, the description also fits both the necromancer of later Greece and the medium who talks with spirits in our own world. If one asks the gods to cast illness upon a person, or madness, or death, this is a malediction in a religious world, an evil spell in another context. The same

difference—or lack of difference—is true of love, which
can be raised in a person thanks to Aphrodite's intervention, or thanks to a drug that has kept its Greek name,
the philter of love, φίλτρον.

Naturally, from the point of view of doctrine, there
is a tremendous difference: in one case, you rely on the
gods and place your hope in them; in the other, you
believe you can bind them, by tricks, to your own con-
venience. Magic, it could be said, breeds on degraded
religion, and its importance grows when religion fades.[25]
Already in the fourth century, Plato is very severe about
the use of drugs and magic tricks, of incantations and
binding spells and wax figures, by which people are led to
believe in fake powers (*Laws* 933a–c). But in a religious
world even magic is religious, or may be so. Circe and
Medea were indeed witches, but Circe was also a god-
dess, and Medea was helped by the sun-god, her ancestor.
There can also be sacred incantations, acknowledged by
the gods. And it will be noted that this is what Gorgias
speaks of: ἔνθεοι . . . ἐπῳδαί. In fact, this accounts for the
difficulty that people have encountered when dealing
with Orphic rites, which appear, according to the
occasion, either as religious or as magical.[26] There
existed, in former time, something that we are entitled
to call sacred magic.

We can see traces of it even in tragedy; for, although
tragedy is no longer regarded as divine or inspired, we
find in it the description and haunting presence of magic
rituals, performed in a religious spirit[27]—particularly,
of course, in Aeschylus.[28] Prayers and maledictions are
frequent in his theater; he shows them taking place, and
he shows them at work.[29] The ἀρά, curse, of Oedipus
against his sons brings inescapable disaster in the *Seven
against Thebes*. Inspired revelations occur, whether in the
case of a special prophet, like Cassandra, or in the case of

the old men of the *Agamemnon*, whose hearts are suddenly possessed by prophetic power (977 ff: "without mission or reward, my song becomes prophet"). Aeschylus also shows us, on the stage, the magic mourning that can call up the dead. The name of such mourning is γόος, which gives us the origin of the word γοητεία, meaning magic. We find such a γόος in the *Persians*, and the result is the appearance of Darius, liberated for a while from the realms of death. We find another in the *Choephori*, giving a feeling that Agamemnon will, from among the dead, help to achieve his own revenge. In these two cases the γόος is a sort of νεκυομαντεία, necromancy. It reminds us of the eleventh book of the *Odyssey*, but also of Lucian's *Menippus*; in both works the very word νεκυομαντεία is given as a subtitle, and in both we have rituals allowing communication between the dead and the living.[30] In Homer they are religious, in Lucian they belong to magic.[31] And who could deny that the song of the Erinyes is a magic song? It is called ὕμνος δέσμιος, a binding song, just as the magic formulas were generally called κατάδεσμα.[32] In later authors, we also find magic rituals used to produce love, as in Theocritus (2) and in Vergil (*Eclogue* 8); and there we find, more precisely still, the idea of tying somebody by a spell (Theocritus in line 10 says καταδήσομαι), not to speak of the magic song, which is more than fifty lines long, addressed to the equally magic ἴυγξ and followed by a long prayer to Selene, which is about a hundred lines long.

Poetry, therefore, does not only resemble magic in the irrational influence it has on people's emotions; it also conveys a lively picture of magic proper, with all the mysterious power of its formulas—a power which it may have been a temptation to emulate.

But that is not all. If we look beyond these literary texts, it soon emerges that there existed another sort of magic, which was more closely related to the power of speech as such and which may more directly account for Gorgias' idea of the magic spell of words. We find the presence of the magic healer.

Healing by incantations has always been important in Greece; it was honored even in the full glory of Hippocratic times.[33] But more important for our theme is that several traditions connect it with poetry and with speech. Orpheus, whom we mentioned among the poets, was a master of incantations and a healer. Nearer to Gorgias, both in time and in place, we find people who may have been to him not only models and examples of sacred healers but also his forerunners in connecting this sacred magic with the power of speech. Gorgias came from Sicily, the country of Empedocles, and he is given by several sources as Empedocles' disciple.[34] We are even told, by a late source, that Gorgias used to tell about the magic cures he had seen Empedocles practicing (γοητεύοντα).[35] And Empedocles was a poet who used inspired style and taught about purifications. Gorgias also lived in a region where Pythagorean teaching was still alive and vigorous.[36] Our image of the master himself is sometimes mixed with features of Orpheus, for both practiced incantations.[37] But tradition[38] tells us a number of things that are both precise and characteristic: that he aimed at curing passions,[39] that he charmed away suffering (ἐκήλει) by his incantations (ἐπῳδαῖς), and that, by his drugs, he calmed emotions (particularly pity and fear).[40] All these documents, although they come from a very late period, suggest the action of speech on the soul. This is what induced Augusto Rostagni to write two important articles, published in 1922, where he tries to detect the existence of a Pythagorean tradition connecting rhetoric with medical magic, or magical medicine.[41] In fact, Empedocles and Pythagoras were considered by some in antiquity as the founders of rhetoric.[42] Gorgias could well have been influenced by a general context of this kind.

It may even be in such circles that the word ψυχαγωγεῖν acquired its new meaning. It was first used for the magic ritual summoning the dead. It is used of the magic γόος that calls up Darius in Aeschylus' *Persians* (687). It is also used for a magician bringing up the dead in Euripides' *Alcestis* (1128).[43] And such was probably the meaning of the word in Aeschylus' play called Ψυχαγωγοί. This meaning never disappeared; it recurs, for instance, in Plato's *Laws* (909b),[44] in Plutarch's *De Sera Numinis Vindicta* (560f), and in Lucian (*Dialogi Deorum* 7.224.1). But the word came to be used for poetry, and particularly for tragedy, which possesses and beguiles the listener's soul—for example, in Isocrates, *To Nicocles* 49 and *Evagoras* 11, and in Aristotle, *Poetics* 1450a. And finally it is used by Plato as providing the exact definition of rhetoric; this is the well-known passage of the *Phaedrus*, 261a: "Would you not call, on the whole, the art of rhetoric a ψυχαγωγία τις, acting through words?"[45] Now it is a fact that the word is used for Pythagoras' action on people by Dicaearchus, quoted by Porphyry.[46] Of course, it may be Dicaearchus' word. However, the very shifting of meaning, whoever started it, illustrates clearly the relation of rhetoric to magic,[47] which commands Gorgias' attitude.

But even though such a tradition may have existed before Gorgias and may have been a factor is his bringing together magic and speech, there is some danger in pressing these suggestions too far—not only because the documents are all so late but because Gorgias completely altered the meaning of this connection. For his aim was a new one, and he laid the emphasis not on magic but on speech.

Pythagoras and Empedocles may have impressed Gorgias and led the way toward the foundation of his rhetoric; but their interest was not rhetoric. Gorgias is a sophist and a skeptic; rhetoric is what interests him. Sacred magic makes its appearance here only to suggest the irrational power of speech. Indeed, what allows magic to come in at all is by no means its value or reality but a severe criticism of language and judgment, and a clear belief in the shortcomings of opinion. These short-comings are rooted in Gorgias' idea that one cannot know reality, an idea present in the *Helen* and proved by the easy changes of opinion in philosophic discussion. This is indeed a deep and audacious analysis, which gives Gorgias' whole program the authority of a complete system.[48]

In that system the very meaning of the power of speech has been transformed. Sacred magic rested on faith; Gorgias' magic rests on the notion that all truth is out of reach. Sacred magic was mysterious; Gorgias' magic is technical. He wants to emulate the power of the magician by a scientific analysis of language and of its influence. He is the theoretician of the magic spell of words.

This is a remarkable claim—and a remarkable shifting from irrational models to rational teaching. Yet I think one can go a little further. We have seen that poetry inspired Gorgias not only in the choice of his aims, but in the very choice of his means. Would it be possible to infer something similar about magic? I think it is, and we may thus come to understand some of the most original features of Gorgias' style and figures.

But what were the means of magic? Magic power itself, being divine, could well remain out of reach. But still, if we look at the documents that we possess, generally through poetic imitation (be it direct, as it is in

Aeschylus, or of a descriptive nature, as in Theocritus and
Vergil), it soon emerges that these rituals and incantations
had in common a certain number of features, as indeed
magic formulas seem to have had at all times and in all
countries.

Among them I could mention the haunting repetition
of words, enhanced by the very clash of their sound. The
Persians already has it, with the insistence on the call,
"you ancient lord, O lord, come, come appear" (657).
The *Choephori* also has it, with the insistence on πάτερ
αἰνόπατερ (315). And to these the Erinyes' song adds such
figures of style as the play on similar forms of words,
equal in length and in structure, and producing an equal
and repeated rhythm: παρακοπά, παραφορὰ φρενοδαλής
(*Eumenides* 330). These combined figures are themselves
turned into a refrain; the παρακοπὰ passage is repeated in
the *Eumenides*, and two other passages, reproducing the
same obstinate rhythm, are similarly repeated in the
following stanzas. In a more religious context, the
prayer that opens the *Agamemnon* uses the same device.
And it must be added that both Theocritus and Vergil
offer proof that this was customary in magic songs. In
Theocritus, ἐπὶ Δέλφιδι δάφναν αἴθω (2.23–24) contains a
pun, and a refrain line is repeated ten times in the first
song, twelve times in the second. The same repetition is
to be found in Vergil, as well as the same play on words
and alliteration: *Ducite ab urbe domun, mea carmina, ducite
Daphnim*.[49]

Now, to return to Aeschylus, it should be kept in
mind that he does not use this style in a folklorish spirit,
but as a direct expression of religious feeling. And it is a
fact that in his ordinary lyrics he borrows, probably with
delight and certainly with success, some of the majesty
belonging to this style.[50] Not to leave the *Persians*, there
is something of liturgical rhyme and repetition in the

complaint of the elders when they mourn, saying:

> Xerxes led them away, popoi,
> Xerxes cast them away, totoi,
> Xerxes drew the mad plan,
> with his seaborne galleys.

These four lines are answered in the antistrophe by a similar repetition, enhanced by the use of the same series of verbs, with ναῖες taking the place of Ξέρξης.[51] Such habits of style may also be compared to Aeschylus' very Greek feeling for the magic meaning of words or proper nouns.[52] Helen's name is suggestive of taking and ruining, and Aeschylus underlines this meaning by calling her ἑλένας, ἕλανδρος, ἑλέπτολις, "the ruin of ships, and men, and the city" (*Agamemnon* 689). In the same play Cassandra complains: Ἀπόλλων, Ἀπόλλων ... ἀπόλλων ἐμός, ἀπώλεσας γάρ ... (1080ff).[53]

This magic atmosphere may be simply liturgical style.[54] As we have seen before, the difference between magic and liturgy in their beginnings was slight. The repeated call of the *Agamemnon* αἴλινον αἴλινον is found again at *Ajax* 627 and *Orestes* 1395; it recalls the Ὑμὴν ὢ Ὑμέναιε of wedding songs, and refrain itself may have been one of the oldest elements of that style.[55] But it has been transferred to magic proper. However, one thing is clear: there existed a liturgical or magical style, which was well alive in Aeschylus' poetry. The examples we have seen may even show us some of its devices, which seem strangely similar to Gorgias' new style and rhetoric.

Professor Finley, when he argued that Gorgias could not claim the privilege of having first used antithesis, wrote that the main features of his style were "punning, wordplay and rhyme."[56] This, indeed, was his originality. Now, is it not a likely inference that these devices, which were meant to subdue the audience and produce in the listeners' souls such and such a feeling, were derived from the wonderful power that they had in magic song and that some poets had already imitated with a thrilling and impressive effect?[57]

When Gorgias uses in the *Epitaphios* formulas like "arrogant for what brings profit, passionate for what is proper, insolent to the insolent, moderate to the moderate, terrible in things terrible," is he not practicing the same kind of incantation, with the same view to a magic spell? Or when he writes in the *Helen* that, if Helen acted as she did, it was "destiny's intention, or the gods' decision, or necessity's compulsion," and that she was ἢ βίᾳ ἁρπασθεῖσα, ἢ λόγοις πεισθεῖσα, ἢ ἔρωτι ἁλοῦσα (even if the last words are missing in the manuscripts), we do not even have to understand what he is saying to realize, from the very sound of the words, that he is imitating the same style.[58]

Here again, such devices were probably used in prose before Gorgias, since they were used in poetry. Yet he was considered in antiquity—for instance, in Diodorus[59] —as having invented them. Why not? This may just mean that he used them more than anybody else and called attention to them, deliberately creating a strange, an elaborate, artificial, jingling style. It may seem to us bad style; and this play on punning and rhyme is easily considered, as already in the fourth century, a brilliant but useless achievement preventing us from paying attention to what is actually said. But we must not forget Thucydides and his great Gorgian figures (even if the influence of Gorgias did not actually prompt him to use them but only encouraged him in so doing): "We love beauty but with simpleness, and philosophy but without weakness" (2.40: φιλοκαλοῦμέν τε γὰρ μετ' εὐτελείας καὶ φιλοσοφοῦμεν ἄνευ μαλακίας). Is this mere play and trickery? Does it spoil our attention or stir it? Does it not suggest, even to the ear, the perfect balance of Athenian civilization as Pericles wishes to show it? It does so by the double combination of opposed virtues, and the very repetition of words of equal length with similar endings. Some may not like it. But there is a sort of spell attached to this artful arrangement of words. And if someone like Thucydides could use it, it could not at that time have seemed a mere fashion, but rather a noble and craftsmanlike device, which could give more powerful impact to some ideas.

Yet the very mention of Thucydides' name suggests another, more serious problem. For it reminds us of the intellectual character of Gorgias' style, and of the great change that these figures underwent when they were transposed from poetry into prose. The sound of words is no longer mysterious; it no longer implies divine intervention or even produces irrational action. It is just style, and an intellectual display of skill. The only thing it appeals to is intellectual surprise, by stirring curiosity, attention, or excitement.

But then, this is only what we might expect; we were aware that Gorgias, while emulating the magician, had a completely different approach. He knew well enough that, with all the pride of a fifth-century man, he was deliberately shifting magic into something rational. And it should be noticed that even his simile does not hold to the irrational nature of magic. He speaks of magic as a τέχνη, an art; and toward the end of the passage it becomes difficult to say whether he is speaking of magic or of science. He repeats that some kinds of speech act in a magic way (ἐφαρμάκευσαν καὶ ἐξεγοήτευσαν), but he also speaks of drugs (φάρμακα) that are meant to develop one humor or another in the human body—a description that fits Hippocratic medicine more than magical drugs.

This connection with medicine does not mean that we have in Gorgias any inkling of Aristotle's catharsis theory, as some scholars have suggested.[60] It is true, of course, that this theory rested on the notion that music and poetry were a sort of medicine,[61] which is not unlike Gorgias. But the need to prove that its action could be salutary arose from Plato's hostility toward this irrational power of poetry and tragedy; it was Aristotle's answer to Plato's criticism, a justification that would have been indifferent to Gorgias, for Gorgias' aim was only practical. Still, what we have in his text is even more important and original. He classifies drugs methodically in order to evolve a clear notion of the various possibilities with which one could reckon. This leads us from the level of magic and incantation to the level of empirical medicine. But it also separates two notions that had long been joined; for, although Gorgias started from inspired poetry and real magic, for his rhetoric he did not count on anything like inspiration. The consequences of this separation were to last a long time. And we should, after Gorgias, draw a firm line between inspiration and elevated style.[62] Gorgias made the glamour of elevated style available to all.

This was a remarkable step on Gorgias' part, and a remarkable conquest. He could be proud of it. Yet his very formulas were, so to speak, charged with dynamite; and, if such was his program, it could easily cause scandal.

Now, perhaps it was not a program at all. I am well aware that the passage from the *Helen* occurs in the context of perfidious speeches such as those that prevailed against Helen's virtue. As Gorgias says, some drugs can cure, others can kill. None the less, his theory is too complete and too eloquently put forward not to have represented, more or less exactly, its author's view about speech and speeches. When he marvels at the power of *logos*, he is certainly sincere; and he certainly admired the fact that man could inspire whatever feelings he wished, with an easy and powerful magic. But the simile was to prove ruinous, both for him and for rhetoric. If I have dwelt so long on it, it is because these images of Gorgias' were to be the starting point of a long and passionate discussion, which went on all through the fourth century and later.

II

Plato and Conjurers

II Rhetoric was bound to meet strong opposition from Plato, and everything in Gorgias' *Helen* about the power of speech seemed to call for that opposition. Speech, Gorgias had said, could be used in different ways—good or bad—just as there are poisonous drugs, and others that heal. Fairly enough, Plato, in his *Gorgias*, remembered that distinction; for his Gorgias says that rhetoric can be used for right or wrong purposes, just as the art of fighting can turn out to be either beneficial or mischievous, according to the use made of it (456c ff). Yet this very neutrality could seem rather dangerous to a moralist like Plato.[1]

But there was something worse. Gorgias had also admitted in the *Helen* that the very principle of the art of speech was to stir passions, and thereby to deceive. It was ἀπάτη. He had established this power of speech on the frailty and uncertainty of human opinion, δόξα.[2] Now nothing was so averse to Plato's passion for accurate knowledge than such an attitude. Indeed, he was severe enough against poets for not being always truthful; he could not approve of rhetoric, when its avowed aim, ἀπάτη, was to falsify truth. Gorgias' reference to poetry, therefore, could not help. On the contrary, it looks very much as if each of these arts inherited, in Plato's eyes, the dangers and shortcomings of the other.[3]

The dangers of rhetoric were even greater, not only because its very principle was deception but because of the direct influence it could have in practical life; the part played by rhetoric in politics during the last thirty years of the fifth century made that danger both obvious and terrifying. Now, the very definition given of rhetoric in Plato's *Gorgias* calls our attention to this political function; for it says that rhetoric deals with the power of persuading the judges in court, the councilors in the Council, and the people in the assembly (452d). And the whole point of the dialogue is to prove that it is better, in the courts of justice, to be punished for one's own faults than to escape punishment and that it is better, in politics, to go against the people's wishes rather than agree with them so as to get their approval. It will even be noticed that the last person to take part in the dialogue—last, but not least—is Callicles, a man whom we do not know and who perhaps never existed; the only thing we can say about him is that he is an ambitious man, who wants, with the help of rhetoric, to grasp power for himself. This is indicative enough of the practical danger of rhetoric. It explains why the notion of tyranny has such an important place in the dialogue (as we see in 466b–e, 470c–471d, which is the part about Archelaus, or 510a–511c, where the aim pursued by Callicles is discussed, not to speak of the fact that in the myth all tyrants are, with Archelaus, condemned to perpetual penance). It also explains why the great men of Athens, known for their skill and success, also fall under criticism; the examples of Pericles, Cimon, Miltiades, and Themistocles are introduced to show that even they pursued the wrong ends: they succeeded in producing ships and walls and power, whereas they should have taught the city not to wish for such unhealthy swelling (517b, 518e). The aim of rhetoric is wrong, not only because it is deceptive but because it has an evil influence.[4]

Plato's attack will develop along very different lines from those of Gorgias' own account of rhetoric. Yet in fact throughout his whole battle with the sophists, Plato turned against them the very analogues on which Gorgias had built his praise of speech. The analogue of poetry had turned out to be dangerous. The analogue of magic turned out to be disastrous; and Plato, with malicious insistence, kept returning to it.

'Aπάτη, or illusion, is the aim of rhetoric. It is also the

aim of magic, when the magician calls up phantoms and makes people believe in things that do not exist. That this is the very principle of rhetoric is obvious. An antilogy, where one speech opposes another, shows that it is possible to see in the same reality now one aspect and now another. Protagoras himself was proud of making the weak thesis strong, and the strong thesis weak. And we all know (thanks to Plutarch, *Pericles* 8) what Thucydides, the son of Melesias, told Archidamus when the Spartan king asked him who was the better fighter, he or Pericles: "When I have knocked him down in a fight," he said, "he argues he didn't fall and wins the fight by persuading the people." That is illusion. To call it also the very nature of magic requires a word of explanation; for such a view can only take place in a general context where magic has been separated from religion. Perhaps there had been too much religious criticism to leave room for sacred magic, and there was too much uncertainty about life not to leave room for tricky witchcraft;[5] credulity generally outlives devotion. Indeed, in the fourth century, we hear no more about trials for impiety, but we do hear about trials for witchcraft, drugs, poison, incantations, and irregular meetings of immoral cults.[6] And it is a fact that the so-called magician could be an object of prosecution.[7] This degradation of what we have called sacred magic is made clear by Walter Burkert's study of the word γόης.[8] It explains why the very notion of magic came to be used with an unfavorable meaning and applied to anything that was deceptive. This meaning already appears in the Hippocratic treatise *On the Sacred Disease* (2), where magic is opposed to religion and piety. It becomes frequent in the fourth century. Callicles, in the *Gorgias*, speaks of the laws of the city, which try to stop the legitimate ambitions of the strongest, calling them γράμματα καὶ μαγγανεύματα καὶ ἐπῳδάς (written formulas and trickeries and spells, 484a). Similarly, when Achilles is condemned as a liar, in the *Hippias Minor*, he is called γόης καὶ ἐπίβουλος (a treacherous imposter, 371a). And Demosthenes is attacked by his rival as being an impostor, a γόης.[9] The new magicians are impostors.

Now Plato, of all people, would be the very last to approve of such practices. His religion was much too pure and ideal for that, and so was his love of reason—hence his joy in using against rhetoric or sophistic the analogue first offered by Gorgias. Indeed, he returns to it over and over again, in order to cast discredit on the ways of the sophists. It may be a general criticism; it is also sometimes a precise one. Such is the case when he hints at their manner of discussing or at their way of beguiling listeners, these two notions being illustrated by the names of two famous magicians of old: Proteus and Orpheus.

Proteus is the symbol of elusive transformation; for, instead of fighting in a direct and honest way, he used to change himself into a number of deceptive forms and shift from one to the other. Now, in a discussion, such a way of behaving is no doubt dishonest, but very effective. And in almost all the dialogues, Socrates keeps complaining that his adversaries shift from one thesis to another in that same shrewd fashion. This is Proteus' trick—or the trick of the sophists.

In the *Republic*, such magic is mentioned in a very interesting context: it is presented as unworthy of the gods and is brought into connection with the two notions normally used for rhetoric—namely, "deceiving" (ἀπατᾶν) and playing on "false impressions" (δοκεῖν). The passage, indeed, deals with the fact that, according to the poets, gods can take different aspects and thus beguile mortals; and it says, at the very start: "Do you believe

God to be a magician (γόητα), appearing [10] as it were on purpose in different forms, now being himself present but changing his figure into different shapes, and now deceiving us and making us believe in such false impressions? Or do you consider him to be simple and never to leave his own form?" (380d). The answer is, of course, that God could not change in that way, for he hates lies. And by and by, after having mentioned the name of Proteus, Plato insists on the conclusion that gods are not to be thought of "as γόητας practicing metamorphosis, nor as leading us astray by lies, whether in words or in deeds" (383a).

Gods do not act so, or should not. But the sophist, whose very aim is to deceive and make us believe and lead us astray by lies, will do just that. In the *Euthydemus*, the two sophists offer an exceptionally sophistic discussion (in the modern meaning of the word *sophistic*). Each thesis is destroyed, one after the other; then one of the assistants, Ctesippus, gets into a rage, but Socrates pacifies the situation by celebrating the astounding skill of the two sophists (θαυμασία σοφία) and suggesting that they were not in earnest: "They were imitating the Egyptian sophist Proteus and using witchcraft (γοητεύοντε ἡμᾶς);[11] so we must imitate Menelaus, and not loose hold of these men before they make an appearance where they are themselves in earnest" (288b–c). That Proteus is called the Egyptian sophist adds to the closeness of the assimilation between him and the sophists; this is a common device in many Platonic similes, where each of the two elements to be compared borrows some of the words belonging to the other.[12]

In other cases, the sophists, or rhetoricians, may not be engaged in a discussion, but in delivering speeches and pouring out words, which have a magical and seductive influence on the audience; here is magic again, only it takes not after Proteus but after Orpheus. Now, in the very beginning of the *Protagoras*, Plato mentions the great number of young foreigners whom Protagoras drags from the cities he has been visiting: he does it by "charming them with his voice, like Orpheus; and they follow him, obeying the charm of his voice" (315a). The fact that the verb κηλεῖν is used twice in two lines is just as revealing as the double assimilation in the *Euthydemus*, and the irony against the sophists is the same. In most cases, however, no specific magician is named, nor is the simile made to bear on such specific habits; Plato just says the sophist is a γόης—and that is enough.

Anything that is irrational and deprives you of lucidity is witchcraft, γοητεία. Anything that suggests an erroneous impression is γοητεία too. This can be shown from two passages in the *Republic*, both of which deal with pleasure. The first deals with pleasure as a spell that deceives man. Plato says (413b–d) that good and sound principles can be taken away from men by theft or charm or violence. This charm, which he mentions with insistence (cumulating the words γοητευθέντες, γοητευθέντας, γοητείας, δυσγοήτευτος), is connected with the notion of being deceived (we find also ἐξαπατῶτο and δυσεξαπάτητον). Let us beware of such "charms"! Plato was deeply conscious of their danger; for, in the *Phaedo* too, he says the soul is beguiled (the word is γοητεύειν) by the body and its pleasures (81b). Now we must not forget that rhetoric also could be accused of leading people astray by aiming at pleasure.

As for the second passage in the *Republic*, it does not deal with the spell of pleasure, but with its relativity. Coming after pain, absence of pain is a pleasure; after pleasure, it is a pain. It is therefore nothing real, only an appearance and a phantasm, γοητεία τις (584a).[13] Again, we are confronted with illusion and reminded that the same argument, thanks to rhetoric, could appear now weaker and now stronger.

These two passages, though they do not deal with rhetoric, show how the simile of magic could be used by Plato against the sophists or orators. Should we be surprised? All arts of illusion are γοητεία. In the *Republic*, so are ἡ σκιαγραφία and ἡ θαυματοποιία, scene-painting and conjuring.[14] Sophists and orators are no better, and their treatment is just as severe. In fact, the condemnation, in their case, is often made clearer and stronger by the addition of other catchwords—some suggesting phantoms, such as εἴδωλα or φαντάσματα, while others introduce a sort of nonfigurative explanation of the simile (among which are μιμητὴς and μίμησις).

In the *Menexenus*, the authors of funeral orations (a type of eloquence marked, no doubt, by the influence of Gorgias) make Socrates feel himself under a spell: γοητεύουσιν ἡμῶν τὰς ψυχάς (235a). He remains listening, taken by a charm (κηλούμενος). The influence of the speech is the result of its sound and of its flattering appeal, which is just as magical as was Protagoras' voice; for Socrates says the words and sounds "ring in my ears and penetrate me so well that only after three or four days can I recover consciousness and find out where on earth I actually am." The simile of magic is used with splendid irony.

In the *Republic*, Socrates speaks of art in general as being an imitation; and he says that whoever pretends he possesses all the practical skills is only deceiving people just as "a magician and imitator" could do (598d: γόητί τινι καὶ μιμητῇ). Here, the word ἀπατᾶσθαι is used twice (598b and d), and the word φάντασμα is also added (598d), so that the condemnation is extremely emphatic.

In the *Sophist*, it is conceded that there may be an art of speech by which the young can be persuaded. And how? Their ears are bound by a charm (234c: γοητεύειν), and they are presented with fake images (εἴδωλα). A long time will then be required to undo their faith in these phantoms (φαντάσματα). The conclusion is that the sophist is a magician (235a: τῶν γοήτων . . . τις) who merely imitates reality. He therefore can be counted among the conjurers (235b: θαυματοποιῶν). Again, later in the same dialogue, his art is connected with all the creators of illusions and wizards (241b: ψευδουργῶν καὶ γοήτων).[15] Even Plato's theory of imitation could gain in clarity by being brought into relation with his hate of conjurers.

However, in the *Politicus*, the man who deals with politics without possessing political knowledge is "the greatest magician of all sophists" (291c: τὸν πάντων τῶν σοφιστῶν μέγιστον γόητα). Such people are to be cast off as being the producers of the greatest phantoms (εἰδώλων), as being "imitators and magicians more than anybody else, and sophists more than any sophist" (303c).

All these examples prove that the three notions of magic, sophistic, and imitation are used by Plato as being almost synonymous. We can therefore feel no surprise when we read in the *Symposium* that love is "a magician and a sophist" (203d: δεινὸς γόης καὶ φαρμακεὺς καὶ σοφιστής) or when we find in the *Laws*, as members of the same group, people who deal with magic, tyrants, orators, leaders, and sophists (908d: μαγγανείαν . . . τύραν-νοι, δημηγόροι, στρατηγοί . . . σοφιστῶν μηχαναί).

The sophists, as is shown by the example of Gorgias, had claimed the wonderful power of magic; they are confuted as practicing the irrational and deceitful art of conjurers.[16] Their very pretense was, for Plato, the key to their undoing.

Yet things are not quite so simple. We are here con-fronted with two baffling circumstances: the first is that the quality of the magician, in Plato, is given not only to the sophists but to Socrates himself; the second is that it is not mentioned at all in the *Gorgias* or in relation to Gorgias himself.

That Socrates is presented as a magician is a well-known fact, and he is so presented in some quite famous similes. Two of them, at least, are *loci classici*.

In the *Meno*, Socrates is compared by Meno to the torpedo or electric fish. This does not sound like magic, but the context is well worth looking at: "Now, it seems to me, you behave with me like a magician, like a wizard, using drugs, and you really beguile me by your incantations, so as to make me feel at a loss" (80a). The three words are γοητεύεις, φαρμάττεις, κατεπᾴδεις; and the cumulative effect is remarkable. Then Meno goes on to explain how surprising his own bewilderment is. And he concludes: "You are wise, I think, not to sail away from here or go abroad, for, if you behaved like that, being an alien in a foreign country, you would soon get put into jail as a magician" (80b: ὡς γόης). This passage confirms that witchcraft was already regarded with distrust and contempt. It also proves that the simile was not just an accident; it is indeed so insistent that, even if it were isolated, it would leave us with a problem.

But it is far from being isolated. In the *Symposium*, Alcibiades draws a well-known comparison between Socrates and Marsyas. Marsyas was as ugly as Socrates; he was a flute player, not a magician, but the context once more brings us back to magic. Marsyas' music used to cast a spell on his listeners: it charmed them (215c: ἐκήλει), so that they were, so to speak, possessed (κατέχε-σθαι). And Alcibiades' view is that Socrates does the same by his mere speech: everybody feels startled and possessed (ἐκπεπληγένοι ἐσμὲν καὶ κατεχόμεθα). Alcibiades even confesses that on such occasions he feels a sort of corybantic ecstasy: his heart beats quickly, he weeps, and his soul is all upset, while nothing of the kind happens when he hears even the best orators. Socrates' influence on his listeners is magical. Alcibiades, as if he wanted to leave us in no doubt about it, adds another simile to the first one. He says the only way to escape is to stop one's ears and run away "as from the Sirens" (216a: ὥσπερ ἀπὸ τῶν Σειρήνων). This brings us back to the very first appearance of the magic arising from music and voice, as we might find it in Homer.

To these famous examples could be added some others. For instance, in the *Republic* (358d), Glaucon thinks Thrasymachus has given in too easily; he has been charmed by Socrates like a serpent under the spell of music: ὥσπερ ὄφις κηληθῆναι. Just as we had the shrewd magic of the sophists, who were conjurers, we have the seductive magic of Socrates, with its mystery. And the parallel goes further. Just as there is a magic charm in pleasure, which beguiles us, there is a magic spell in noble speeches, which act upon the soul so as to cure it. This is said in the *Charmides* (157a), where the word *incantation* (ἐπῳδή) is used four times in succession and is connected, as it was in Gorgias, with the word φάρμακον. Similarly, in the *Republic*, whereas the magic spell of poetry is acknowledged and its danger described by the word κηλεῖσθαι (607d), the necessity of resisting this charm is put forward, and the very *logos* that will help resist it is called an incantation (608a: ἐπᾴδοντες τοῦτον τὸν λόγον καὶ ταύτην τὴν ἐπῳδήν).[17]

We could add to these passages the different texts where the *logos*, or the text of the laws, is called a φάρμακον. Is that magic, or medicine? Who could tell? It may depend on cases. And we must remember that, in the *Helen*, we had already seen, toward the end, a curious hesitation between both, with the distinction

34

between good drugs, which could cure, and bad drugs, intended to kill. After all, this very ambiguity is rooted in the empiric (and magical) nature of early medicine.[18] For Plato, of course, there is a great difference. In the *Laws* (933c), he speaks of the danger of giving drugs (φαρμάττειν) without a real knowledge of medicine, or of using magic charms without being a seer. However, we do find a good φάρμακον in the dialogues. Sometimes, to make things clearer, Plato calls it ἀλεξιφάρμακον,[19] as in *Alcibiades I* 132b and *Laws* 957c–958a. In other cases, the context is clear because the φάρμακον is actually given by a doctor (so in *Charmides* 155d). But the meaning is obviously the same wherever virtuous advice or a sound argument is said to act as a φάρμακον, capable of curing evil and breeding wisdom (so, particularly, in *Politicus* 310a and in the *Charmides*).

One can, of course, deal with such passages by considering that they do not imply any sort of magic, but only good and sound medicine. The ambivalent meaning of the word allows such an interpretation. Scholars may even try to elicit a theory about the ambivalent nature of the φάρμακον. Jacques Derrida has built an original theory, according to which the bad φάρμακον is writing, whereas *logos* is the antidote.[20] However that may be, we can get rid of the passages about φάρμακον. But, then, what about the ἐπῳδή?

Naturally, if we want to get rid of the ἐπῳδή, we can. The metaphor, in the context of the two passages quoted, is made much easier by the presence either of an actual medical treatment, such as the treatment of headache in the *Charmides*, or of an actual spell, such as the spell of poetry in the *Republic*. This could account for the metaphor and suggest that it is just occasional. Still, it is a little annoying to have to get rid of too many things. And after such dubious efforts we should still have the magician himself: we should still have Socrates. So we must face the problem: how can the passages about him be reconciled with the deprecatory use made of the same simile against the sophists? What does this double application mean?

I think the problem might be clarified by a closer examination of Socrates' magic—which, in fact, is something quite different from the magic of the sophists. It rests, obviously, on the combination of two very different qualities that Socrates combined. First, how could we forget that Socrates had a sort of divine quality about him? What he calls the demonic voice is, indeed, inspiration of some sort; and it is not wholly different from the obscure certainty that the chorus in the *Agamemnon* experiences about the impending disaster. It is perhaps less mysterious, less irrational, and closer to moral intuition. Yet, it is not moral intuition only; for it implies piety and constant devotion and direct dependence on the will of God. It is indeed a sort of irrational power, but a power that arises from a close contact with the divine. This inspiration may therefore resemble a magician's gift, except that it has nothing to do with the sophists' magic.

But, practically, what puzzles people about Socrates is not this mysterious inspiration; it is the way he discusses, clinging to reason and truth, and trying to do away with all fake appearances, all unsound arguments or definitions. Those who complain that they cannot resist him, or cannot see where they stand after having discussed with him, are merely bewildered by the power of thorough analysis. They do not understand what happens to them, but we do: they are just confronted with unyielding logic. Whereas the magic of the sophists aimed at producing illusion, Socrates' magic rests on the obstinate destruction of all illusions. It is the magic of implacable truth; and certainly it is not just by chance that those who describe that magic spell of Socrates are young men or laymen, not used to thorough reasoning, men such as Meno and Alcibiades.

It is therefore one magic against another, the one taking the former's place, but with opposite aims and means. This very parallelism between the two series of texts thus becomes illuminating. It shows clearly enough that in Greece rational and irrational were often combined; so they were in Gorgias, so they were in Socrates, so they were in Plato, who could use so well the magic seduction of style and imagery. But, what is even more important, it shows how deeply these Greeks of the fifth century were, at all levels, enthralled by the power of speech. Gorgias represented the deceiving power of style, or of the choice and arrangement of arguments, which could create at will any kind of emotion. Socrates represents the stimulating power of reasoning and discussion, when devoted to the search for truth. But in both cases this power was bewildering, amazing, magical. The Greeks were lost in wonder at the marvel of the instrument they were learning to master.

This external similarity explains, in a way, how Socrates could be mistaken for one of the sophists; but it also brings to light the radical opposition between his aim and theirs, between his means and theirs. The new magic was the answer to the first one, and Plato was perfectly coherent when, after laughing at the sophists as conjurers, he drew this splendid portrait of his wonderful and disturbing master.

Once we are free of this first difficulty, we can also understand, I hope, the other puzzling circumstance that I have mentioned, namely, that Plato never used the simile of magic while discussing Gorgias.[21] Magic and all the tricks of the sophists or stylists could be made fun of. But Gorgias' personal case was different. If only he had been but a conjurer! In fact, what made him dangerous was that he had turned this magic into something that could be taught and could deceive people in all sorts of situations, mainly in the field of justice and politics. He had succeeded, and the change in Athenian politics was his doing, not because he himself was a conjurer but because he had claimed that this rhetoric of his was something serious, a τέχνη, and because everybody had followed him. Plato resented not the magic, but the offensive pretense of turning it into science.

Now this had been Gorgias' boast. In §10 of the *Helen*, the word τέχνη appears in the same sentence that deals with magic: he says that two τέχναι have been found for magic, the one resting on the soul's being in error, the other on the deception of judgment (ψυχῆς ἁμαρτήματα καὶ δόξης ἀπατήματα, another play on words!). Further along in the same passage (§13), he alludes to a speech τέχνῃ γραφείς, written with art.[22] Finally, in a passage already mentioned, he speaks of φάρμακα developing one humor or another in the body, that is to say, of the art of medicine.[23] The art of speech is not only magic but something technical, and even scientific. That was Gorgias' originality. That was the discovery of rhetoric, ἡ ῥητορικὴ τέχνη. And that was what Plato could not condone.

The choice of characters and the order in which they appear in the *Gorgias* dramatize in an illuminating way the danger implied in rhetoric and the consequences it could have. The first part of the dialogue is a discussion between Socrates and Gorgias himself, showing that rhetoric does not aim at truth. The second part is a discussion between Socrates and Polus, Gorgias' disciple, showing that therefore rhetoric is not a τέχνη but a low practice aiming at flattery and pursuing an advantage that is, in fact, an evil. The third part is a discussion between Socrates and Callicles, a figure who represents the ambitious young statesmen who used Gorgias' rhetoric in order to fulfill their own longing for power; this part shows that the very aim of fulfilling such an ambition is a wrong aim, which should never be entertained, for it ruins the only desirable end, which is justice.

The very movement of the dialogue, therefore, shows with what skill Plato could shift a problem from one level to another. Gorgias has only to acknowledge that he does not teach truth or justice; the implications and consequences of such a position are then searched through other people, less and less close to Gorgias, and considered from a wider and wider point of view. The danger is not rhetoric but the philosophy implied by the pursuit of rhetoric.

It is not less illuminating to observe that, throughout this development, the notion of τέχνη is prominent; it is treated from different angles, so that the discussion seems to reach higher and higher, leaving rhetoric well behind. In the first section, it bears only on the nature of the τέχνη that Gorgias teaches and on its proper field; [24] the conclusion is embarrassing, for rhetoric deals with justice but does not teach justice; or does it? The very embarrassment suggests that rhetoric has no proper field of real knowledge. In the second section, Socrates goes further and boldly states that rhetoric is not a τέχνη at all (462b: οὐδεμία ἔμοιγε δοκεῖ). It is practical skill, similar to cooking, and it is, like cooking, some low kind of flattery, but no τέχνη (463a: τεχνικὸν μὲν οὔ; 465: τέχνην δὲ αὐτὴν οὔ φημι εἶναι). In the discussion with Callicles, the same idea is repeated (500b, e, 501b, 503a, d); but it is also extended to the realm of politics. Rhetoric is the means of the common statesman, but Socrates is one of the rare men, or perhaps the only man, to practice true πολιτικὴ τέχνη (521d).

Socrates' argument is an insistent rejection, an obstinate defense against Gorgias' dangerous success. Plato made a similar attack upon rhapsodes and poets, in the little dialogue called the *Ion*, where he says that they may well act under divine inspiration but certainly have no lucid knowledge, or τέχνη.[25] Rhetoric and poetry are once more treated alike. But what is an innocent teasing in the case of poetry is an unrelenting attack in the case of rhetoric, for rhetoric had higher pretentions and presented much greater danger.

The dangerousness of rhetoric accounts not only for the structure of the dialogue but for the choice of the image that seems to command the whole discussion. The image is not magic but medicine, which also occurred in Gorgias' *Helen*, where he suggested toward the end of the passage mentioned above that rhetoric was, in a way, similar to medicine.

Such a parallel, of course, may have been natural, in view of the parallelism of soul and body, which plays an important part in the opening of the *Protagoras* (312b ff). But it was also something that must have appealed to Gorgias. It offered him a place for his magic, since medicine had started in close union with magic. It offered him also a stimulating catchword, since medicine was at that time the great field of scientific progress. It had a special meaning for him personally too, since his brother was a doctor. But precisely because it revealed his ambition, the assimilation of rhetoric to medicine was to prove unfortunate, and even more so than the witchcraft simile. Plato seems unable to refrain from returning over and over again to the idea that rhetoric has nothing to do with medicine; his dialogue can be read as an obstinate and passionate refusal of such a parallelism.

The very first question he asks about the nature of rhetoric is framed around a contrast with medicine, and an allusion is made to the fact that Gorgias' brother was a doctor (448b). Then, when it has been admitted that rhetoric deals with speeches, Socrates asks what particular speeches, again introducing a contrast with medicine (450a).[26] Then, when Gorgias boasts that the speeches he deals with bear on the greatest and best things in human life, the discussion suggests that this could be said of medicine (452a). And, when Gorgias wants to explain how wonderful rhetoric is, he boldly asserts that, were he, with his brother, by the side of a patient, the patient would listen to him, not to his brother the doctor (456b). All that, of course, leads us to understand, progressively, that rhetoric does not rest on actual knowledge. Indeed, toward the end of the first section, Gorgias admits that the man who has learned rhetoric could persuade an audience, about any matter, better than the specialist—among whom the doctor is again the first to be mentioned—and this although the rhetorician knows nothing of technical matters (459a–b). Medicine rests on knowledge, rhetoric does not.

It is no surprise, therefore, to see that, in the second section, when Plato wants to classify the real arts and the fake ones, he once more starts with medicine as a real art (464a) and draws a strong opposition between such arts and rhetoric. The contrast with medicine recurs a number of times in this second section (467c, 477e–478a). It also assumes a new meaning, for Socrates insists that rhetoric does not provide a real good, whereas medicine does. Doctors' treatments are not agreeable, but they are useful (478b–c). Therefore, one should pity the man who does not go to see a doctor and suffer what the doctor wants him to suffer in order to be cured (478d–480d). By such an argument Socrates progressively puts forward his great rule of life, which is the undoing of rhetoric, and of its very aim: I mean the idea that it is better, when one is at fault, to be punished and cured than to escape punishment and remain with an evil soul or a sick one. The action of medicine is good; the action of rhetoric is not. And the example of medicine, which Gorgias wanted to emulate, is used to refute his claim.

Now it would seem that in the last section, which is less technical and less oriented toward definitions, this continued contrast should fade away; but it does not. It is often recalled as an important part of Socrates' doctrine (490b, 501a, 504c, 505a, 514d). What is more remarkable still, now that the interest turns toward politics and ambition, the contrast between rhetoric and medicine again provides the key to the new discussion: rhetoric and its use in politics only produce an unhealthy swelling (518e–519a), whereas doctors always act for the good of the people (517d–518a). Even Socrates' condemnation, which is foreshadowed in the dialogue, is explained by the fact that those who will accuse or judge him have no real knowledge of what is good in politics: he is like a doctor, attacked by a cook and judged by a court of children (521d–522c). The accusers of Socrates were, of course, people trained in rhetoric. So here we reach the ultimate contrast between rhetoric, which ruins political life, and an art like medicine (we can call it πολιτικὴ τέχνη), which alone could save it.

Finally, even in the myth, the same contrast is present; for the whole point of the punishments in hell is that they can cure people of their sins, or, in the worst cases, help others to recover moral health and sanity.

Rhetoric, therefore, is always treated—whether one considers its subject matter or its aim or its use in politics—as contrary to medicine. To be a conjurer could be condoned; to be a conjurer acting as a doctor and treated as one was intolerable. That this criticism of Plato's was paving the way for the foundation both of dialectic as a search of truth, and of political science as an ideal, is obvious; it is important also to see that, in launching these ideas, the direct controversy with Gorgias had been of so much help and influence.

But this controversy was only the opening of a wide discussion, which was to go on for the whole century and even longer. Severe as it had been, the *Gorgias* was in no way the ruin of rhetoric. There were answers, rectifications, arguments of all sorts. Now, although I have insisted on the contrast with medicine, I have not considered in detail the classification of the four arts and the four fake arts that is put forward in the middle part of the dialogue (464 ff). I have not done so because the discussion of that matter has been particularly precise and continuous and provides a good example of the manner in which the Greeks held a sort of perpetual dialogue, where each author answers his predecessor with precision and subtlety. This we shall see in the next chapter. But now we must prepare for a short parting with one of our two themes—the theme of magic. Plato had laughed at the conjurers, offered the example of another, greater magic, and attacked rhetoric as being no $\tau\acute{\epsilon}\chi\nu\eta$. In order to save rhetoric as a $\tau\acute{\epsilon}\chi\nu\eta$, in order to keep some room for it in the classification of $\tau\acute{\epsilon}\chi\nu\alpha\iota$, one had to ignore all connection with magic. The great argument of Plato, finally, could be put into these simple terms: "You can't be both." Perhaps he was right. But he weighed heavily, not only on the status of rhetoric but on its development, and on literary taste itself, which was more serious. It is his fault that we have to say, for a while, farewell to the magicians.

III

Rhetoric and the
Classification of Arts in the
Fourth Century B.C.

III This chapter—as the title suggests—will be austere and technical. It will contain no more magic, and it will deal with texts that may appear slightly obsolete. Who cares, nowadays how the different τέχναι were classified? The question may seem to us an academic one, which we moderns are wise enough to have abandoned. Yet it is interesting to investigate; and, by way of antidote, I shall first explain why. It is not only because one may like the intellectual game of seeing how things worked and explaining thereby the changes from one author to another. It is partly because, even if the problem at stake does not interest us directly, it is stimulating to observe how the Greeks could conduct through a whole century a serious and continuous discussion in which texts answer one another and ideas take progressively more precise shape. It is also because all through that discussion with rhetoric as a starting point several disciplines gradually came to be defined, disciplines that we still know as such, programs of education that still linger behind our own efforts in that field.

All that because Gorgias had seemed to suggest that there was some parallel between rhetoric and medicine, and Plato had been shocked! For this was the simple, formal problem that opened such a long and varied discussion. Before we follow its actual course, in order to clarify its meaning we must recall Plato's exact position as it appears not only in the *Gorgias* but in the *Phaedrus*. Thus we may throw some light on the replies given to him by other authors; it seems in fact fairly obvious that Isocrates answers the *Gorgias* while Aristotle answers the *Phaedrus*.[1]

In the *Gorgias*, not only does Plato draw an obstinate distinction between the aims of rhetoric and those of medicine, but he is so eager to leave no doubt about their difference that he offers his readers a complete classification of arts, which he develops from 464b to 466a and recalls in several other passages, mainly 500d–501c.[2]

He starts by adopting Gorgias' parallel between soul and body; but by an initial energetic rectification he states that the art that deals with the soul is not rhetoric but politics (πολιτικὴν καλῶ). As for the body, its art is not medicine alone but gymnastic and medicine (the first preparing the body to be healthy, the second curing it when it is not). Now this clear subdivision about the body has its parallel as regards the soul: legislation prepares the soul to be just, and corrective justice (in lawsuits and sanctions)[3] cures it when it is not. Between each of the arts dealing with the soul, and each of the arts dealing with the body, there is thus a correspondence: they are parallel and correlative, or to use the Greek word ἀντίστροφοι.

So far, all is clear and neat. But it will be noticed that rhetoric does not come in at all. Before it can come in, Plato draws a second new distinction. To him, medicine and rhetoric were the arts, the only ones. But flattery now enters and invents spurious arts, which aim only at pleasure. While the art of medicine enables us to have healthy food, which is good for us, the art of cooking, aiming at pleasure, enables us to have agreeable food, which may well be unhealthy. Among these spurious arts we shall find rhetoric. But even there it will have nothing to do with medicine. It deals with the soul, not the body; and it aims at pleasure, not at the good; it therefore has a completely different position. For we finally get a complete classification of eight arts, all corresponding to one another according to the different point of view that is adopted: for the body, gymnastic and medicine, with their counterfeits, the art of the cosmetician and dressmaker on the one hand, the art of cooking on the other; for the soul, legislation and corrective justice, with their counterfeits, sophistic and rhetoric. Yes, these twin arts, sophistic and rhetoric, the proud discoveries of Gorgias and his friends, are reduced to the level of cooking and adorning one's person—lost, unscientific, dangerous, and low. They teach nothing, they aim at nothing good. The new line that has been drawn by Plato has resulted in their being banished from among the real τέχναι more effectually than their friend poetry could ever be banished from Plato's ideal city.

Now this new arrangement is so brilliant that it ought to have been final. But it was not. It could have been sufficient against rhetoric as it was taught by the sophists in the fifth century B.C., but then a man appeared, who had been, or was supposed to have been, a disciple of Socrates on the one hand, of Gorgias and Theramenes on the other (Theramenes himself being a disciple of Gorgias).[4] This man opened a new school of rhetoric, where he professed to give complete moral instruction. Indeed, he proudly called this rhetorical teaching "philosophy." And he was extremely successful. He was so anxious to clear rhetoric of all the sins denounced by Plato that one of the first pamphlets in which he advertised his new rhetoric was called *Against the Sophists*. This may have appeared around 390, shortly after or shortly before the *Gorgias*. However, he was obviously opening a new perspective, which could save rhetoric— as, in fact, it did. For he did not keep to Gorgias' neutral attitude toward virtue and morality: he said that he did not believe virtue could be taught, but that it could receive great help and be sustained by the practice of political eloquence (*Against the Sophists* 21).

This claim may well explain why Plato later had to come back to rhetoric, as he did fifteen or twenty years after the *Gorgias*, when he wrote the *Phaedrus*. In the *Phaedrus*, he cannot focus, as he did before, on the aim of rhetoric; for he is now fighting a man who insists that he does aim at what is good, approved of, and thoroughly useful. Therefore we find in the *Phaedrus* a shift in the way rhetoric is criticized. It is still not an art. But the reason is not that it aims at pleasure; its fault is that it does not rest on real knowledge. In dealing with all the famous authors of $T\acute{\epsilon}\chi\nu\alpha\iota$, Plato asserts that the programs of instruction they provide are not a $\tau\acute{\epsilon}\chi\nu\eta$. He goes back to the old example of drugs, which can produce such and such a result in the human body; knowledge of these results, to him, is no scientific medicine, any more than the capacity to write a *rhesis* is the art of tragedy, or the knowledge of how to produce one note or another with an instrument is the art of music. In each case, only a low practical experience is involved, and the same is true for rhetoric: all the teachings of the masters may have to be learned if one wants to study rhetoric, but they do not constitute real rhetoric. Finally there seems to be a "real" rhetoric, and it seems to be respectable; only it is a rhetoric that has not yet come into being.

Now it is clear why, suddenly, Plato comes back to the parallel between medicine and rhetoric. He might seem to be returning to Gorgias' scheme, but that would be an illusion. Neither Plato's medicine nor Plato's rhetoric have anything to do with Gorgias' medicine and rhetoric. Plato's medicine (time has elapsed and personal choice has made some features more essential) rests not on any practical experience about the action of drugs but on a rational analysis of the nature of the body, as part of a rational notion about the whole universe. With emphatic reference to the name of Hippocrates,[5] Plato explains how such an analysis must proceed: it must ask whether the thing under consideration is simple or not, what are its properties (δύναμις), what can be done by it or to it, and so on (270b–d). Similarly, rhetoric should rest on a serious knowledge about the nature of the soul and about the means by which anything can be done by it or to it; also, it should make a thorough classification of the different kinds of *logoi* and of the different kinds of souls. The program goes on similarly for two pages, in a sort of abstract, administrative certainty (271d: ἔστιν οὖν τόσα καὶ τόσα, καὶ τοῖα καὶ τοῖα, ὅθεν οἱ μὲν τοιοίδε οἱ δὲ τοιοίδε γίγνονται . . .).

But, ultimately, what is such a complete and lucid knowledge? What, if not philosophy, nay, dialectic? Just a few pages before, Plato had given one of his descriptions of dialectic, with its twin movement, one upward, aiming at unity and seeking the Idea, the other downward, following all the natural divisions that lead from the general to the particular. Now, Plato requires from rhetoric a similar effort: one movement climbing upward in search of the nature of the soul, and another descending into a correct division and classification of all particulars. And, when he has described this double movement, he acknowledges, in a very honest way, that ultimately it is not worth while merely for the sake of speeches; it is worth while only for the sake of truth and of winning the approval of the gods (273e–274a).

What Isocrates called "philosophy," which meant learning how to be a reasonable and useful citizen, consisted, for him, in learning how to speak well. For Plato, we have the reverse: what he calls "rhetoric" (which does not yet exist) was but a low and second-rate offspring of philosophy, which meant learning the truth by means of dialectic. Both words (*rhetoric* and *philosophy*) have changed level. Isocrates gives a lower meaning to philosophy in order to make it synonymous with rhetoric; Plato gives a higher meaning to rhetoric in order to bring it nearer to philosophy.

Also, this very change of level enables Plato to dispose of Gorgias for the second time. Indeed, he seems to keep the former parallel that Gorgias had established between medicine and rhetoric. But Gorgias' medicine and Gorgias' rhetoric were both magical, and practical, and therefore of no value; the genuine parallelism between the genuine arts leaves him completely behind, in the vague suburbs of training and propaideutic. The change of level is here even more radical than when we were comparing Plato with Isocrates, and it affects both medicine and rhetoric.

The *Phaedrus* ought to have been the undoing of rhetoric. But, once more, it was not. Rhetoric of course never died, with the Greeks. In fact, it survived in the fourth century thanks to the obstinate, rival efforts of Isocrates and Aristotle, whose task was to liberate rhetoric from the irrational commitments of the old sophist and to disallow his magic at all costs. Thus both of them were led, by the very necessity of polemics, to suggest new and different classifications of the various τέχναι.

Isocrates can be understood only by reference to Gorgias. Like Gorgias, he wrote a praise of the *logos*. The text is famous. And it is found twice in Isocrates' work (*Nicocles* 5–9 and *Antidosis* 253–257); so he held it as important.[6] But the way he wrote that praise is as different from Gorgias' way as his praise of Helen is different from Gorgias' *Helen*. He does not try to white-wash Helen, as in a lawsuit, by showing that it was not her fault if she acted as she did; that was what Gorgias had done. Isocrates chooses in Helen's life what can be noble and worthy of praise, or what turned out to be useful for the Greeks. He does not discuss, but searches for what is good and preaches about it. In the same manner, he does not praise the power of speech for the psychological influence that it can have on an audience and that can be used, at will, for the better or for the worse; he starts from a general view of speech as the privilege of mankind and considers it as the vehicle of thought and, therefore, as the means of bringing out all the progress man can achieve toward a civilized way of life.

The originality of this view appears even more clearly if we remember that, according to Protagoras, the special privilege of man, which allowed him to achieve progress and live in a civilized way, was virtue, or, more precisely, αἰδὼς and δίκη, which were the roots of πολιτικὴ τέχνη (*Protagoras* 322b–c); this was what enabled man to create cities and maintain their unity. And, combined with the gift of fire, which fostered the invention of arts and crafts, these virtues accounted for civilization. Now Isocrates follows the same pattern and mentions the same achievements; but they all now come from the *logos*: "Because we developed the possibility of persuading each other about what we want, not only have we got rid of a savage manner of life but, by coming to live together, we have created cities, established laws, and discovered arts and crafts." *Logos* is indeed a decisive substitution for the δίκη of Protagoras' pattern; there is also a decisive change in the way of praising the *logos*, and one that Cicero was to adopt.[7] We are here very far from Gorgias' magic used to create artificial emotions!

But how can the *logos* do all that Isocrates says it does? Here again Isocrates, in a way, resembles Gorgias. All his philosophy rests, as does that of Gorgias, on opinion, δόξα. Whereas Plato could be satisfied only by knowledge and science, Isocrates does not believe in the possibility of reaching such certainty. He writes (*Antidosis* 184) that by his teaching his disciples will form opinions (δόξαι) that will correspond more closely to actual circumstances. He insists later in the same speech (271): "Since it is not in the nature of man to be able to acquire a science (ἐπιστήμη) by which we should know how to act or speak, I consider as wise (σοφοί) those who, by their opinions (δόξαι) are able in most cases to hit on what is best, and as philosophers those who train themselves in order to acquire such wisdom." Gorgias, with his insistence on δόξα and the frailty of human judgment, would have been pleased. But Gorgias had never thought or claimed that this δόξα could be trained so as to bring men nearer to truth and virtue.

How can it? Isocrates built a whole philosophy to answer that question. It can, because to him the test of all truth or virtue lies in what wins men's approval. In discussion, we come nearer to truth, or to what can be admitted by all as such. In action, if we want to be approved of, we must behave according to virtue, that is to say, what is considered by all as such. All that we have is δόξα, but the fact that it is not private but rests on general agreement gives it more value and even provides a kind of objectivity.[8] Therefore Isocrates' δόξα stands in a median position between Gorgias' skepticism and Plato's ambitious claim to rational and pure knowledge.

Thus Isocrates can write in his praise of *logos* some proud statements that closely connect speech with morality and wisdom: "Speech has fixed the rules regarding what is just and unjust, shameful or beautiful"; and later: "Thanks to speech, we educate the fools and put the wise to test; for we consider the fact of speaking rightly as the greatest sign of correct thinking." Virtue and truth are thus attained—not of course in their pure and absolute perfection, but, as he writes in *Antidosis* 84, in the form "on which everybody agrees."

If the *logos* in general can achieve such results, the use of *logos*, in its most humble and practical way, can also stimulate intellectual and moral virtues. If the orator wants to impress the audience will he not need the help of appealing themes and personal morality? And "the more one wishes to persuade the audience, the more one will try to have a favorable reputation among one's fellow citizens" (*Antidosis* 278: εὐδοκιμεῖν). At all levels speech, truth, and virtue go hand in hand; and teaching one means teaching the others. By such a thorough correction of Gorgias' views, Isocrates could indeed answer Plato's criticism against rhetoric; for his aim was to give by means of rhetoric a real training of man, a παιδεία, which would make people better.

Therefore magic had nothing more to do with his rhetoric. It is even remarkable to see how carefully Isocrates avoids all words connected with magic. He believed in the *logos*, he believed in style and figures and talent; but he was loyal to his ideal of παιδεία, and so he never uses γοητεία (or γόης) or μαγεία, nay, not even κηλεῖν or θέλγειν or θελκτήριον.[9] He is hostile to the idea of mixing rhetoric with anything like magic, and this very silence is an eloquent testimonial.

But then, might he not return to Gorgias' attempted parallel between rhetoric and medicine? He almost did. Yet, once more, while going back to Gorgias' position, he also corrected Gorgias, in the light of Plato's criticism. In *Antidosis* 181ff, he draws a new parallel between the arts that deal with the soul and those that deal with the body. At first sight, it would seem that neither rhetoric nor medicine has any place there. Yet by close attention we can see that rhetoric is there, in full sight. But, it has acquired a new importance, a new dimension: since it is now claiming to teach wisdom, it has received a new name, "philosophy." This "philosophy," Isocrates says a few lines below, teaches its disciples the art of speech. And medicine? It is true that medicine has disappeared, and rightly so. Plato had shown in the *Gorgias* that preparing a body to be healthy is a different matter altogether from curing it when it is not; he had called the first art gymnastic. How could Isocrates, who was such a passionate addict of παιδεία and who pretended that his rhetoric was the best kind of παιδεία, ignore such a difference? His own parallel will be, therefore, between philosophy (that is, rhetoric) and gymnastic. But, lest that sound a little low and limited, he again adds a slight correction: "the art of the physical trainer, of which gymnastic is a part" (181). He probably means that the physical trainer also teaches courage and discipline, looks after the children's food, and so on. After all, Plato himself, in the *Republic* (410b), admitted that a young man trained in music, if he studied gymnastic, would no longer be in need of a doctor.

Thanks to these two slight changes (one correcting Plato's hostility to the value of rhetoric, the other making use of Plato's distinction between gymnastic and medicine),[10] Isocrates can recover a sound and firm parallel between his rhetoric and physical training. He insists with proud obstinacy that he can do it. Plato had used the word ἀντίστροφοι for the parallelism that he had accepted, in the *Gorgias*, between the real arts dealing with the soul on the one hand and the body on the other; Isocrates borrows it in his own classification, saying that his teaching and physical training are parallel, or ἀντίστροφοι; and he accumulates a whole series of other words that give it increased importance, for he calls them ἀντιστρόφους καὶ σύζυγας καὶ σφίσιν αὐταῖς ὁμολο-γουμένας (182).

He also uses this new and precise parallel in order to describe his own method. First, in both fields, one teaches the general elements (οἱ μὲν παιδοτρίβαι teaching

the σχήματα, those concerned with physical training teaching the figures; οἱ δὲ περὶ τὴν φιλοσοφίαν ὄντες teaching the
ἰδέας, those concerned with philosophy teaching the ideas).
Then, in both fields, one trains the pupils by practical
exercise until they improve, here in their judgment, there
in their physical dispositions. The limits, in both fields,
are also the same; for neither of these two sorts of teachers
(185: οὐδέτεροι) can succeed in making of any given
person here a perfect athlete and there a good orator.
They can only help develop the natural qualities of
each one in his own field.

In insisting so much on the part played by practical
training and on the importance of natural gifts, Isocrates
no doubt answers and corrects the boast of some of the
sophists, as is apparent from his early treatise *Against the
Sophists*, in which similar ideas are put forward, as well
as from some subsequent developments of the *Antidosis.*[11] But, in describing the result, he is answering and
correcting Plato. One and the same pattern, or parallel,
thus helps him to establish his original position between
two extremes.

All this thorough and subtle polemic, resting on sound
analysis, comes out in small details: in the use of one
word instead of another, in a slight change within a
classification that seems almost identical. A whole philosophy commands the unobtrusive details of apparently
innocent sentences.

This should be a lesson in how to read the classics. It
is also a good answer to those who think Isocrates never
does much more than insist on the obvious. In the present
case, it ought to be noted that even Plato understood the
meaning of this effort by Isocrates to turn rhetoric into a
παιδεία worthy of that name, as is probably revealed by
allusions in his second dialogue on rhetoric, the *Phaedrus*.

There we find, toward the end, a mitigated judgment
on Isocrates, colored with irony: speaking as of the

dramatic date of the dialogue, Plato says about him that there is by nature some philosophy in the man's mind (279a: φιλοσοφία τις) and that it would not be surprising if, with time, he could grow up to surpass people like Lysias. Isocrates, when the *Phaedrus* was written, was already an old man, and he was not likely to change what had been a determined endeavor of his whole long life. Plato, therefore, means only that, although Isocrates had some inkling of the fact that rhetoric should aim at some kind of truth and virtue, neither his aim nor his method could be compared with real philosophy or, indeed, with real rhetoric.

Isocrates' effort to save rhetoric and clear it of all suspicion was to remain a success for centuries to come, but it was not sufficient for Plato, who could not be satisfied by such a modest and pedestrian notion of philosophy.

Was it not possible to do more? Was it not possible to have a purer rhetoric and to emulate Isocrates' teaching—his successful teaching—with another, which would be more in line with Plato's ideal and more immune from his criticism? After all, Plato himself did write in the *Phaedrus* of an ideal rhetoric. Perhaps it could exist. And this is where Aristotle comes in.

When Isocrates wrote the *Antidosis*, Aristotle had been in Athens for twelve or thirteen years. He left Athens shortly before Isocrates' death (338). And it is obvious that, in his works, he often criticizes his master Plato, and also Isocrates.[12] In fact, just as Isocrates had chosen a place between Gorgias and Plato, Aristotle, in so far as rhetoric is concerned, chooses a place between Isocrates and Plato.

At first, he may have shared Plato's severity toward rhetoric; for in the *Gryllus* he seems to have said that rhetoric had no field of its own and no other aim than to please the audience.[13] But some years later he wrote his *Rhetoric*, where it became obvious that he was interested in teaching rhetoric, like Isocrates, but that he understood under that name something very different from Isocrates' notion and much closer to Plato's ideal.

In the *Phaedrus*, authentic rhetoric was described as something not yet existing, and its method was described in terms of what it ought to be. Now, if we look at the structure of Aristotle's *Rhetoric*, we can see clearly that he followed his master's suggestion. In the first book, he lists and classifies the different sorts of speeches and what they are about. In the second book, he starts with the idea that speeches are meant to act on the dispositions of the audience, and he enters a new classification, that of the different emotions ($\pi\acute{a}\theta\eta$, 1–11) and dispositions of characters ($\mathring{\eta}\theta\eta$, 12–17). This seems to conform to Plato's scheme.[14]

Also, Aristotle's whole treatise rests on an analysis of what kind of reasoning lies at the root of rhetoric; it develops along the line of his logic and contains, both before the classification of speeches and after the classification of emotions and characters, a discussion of the kind of logic used in rhetorical demonstration. This addition could, at first sight, seem to be a reinforcement of Plato's teaching, giving it a more rationalistic basis. Yet this very reinforcement implies quite a number of slight changes and rectifications.

First, if rhetoric is to be studied according to its manner of reasoning, it becomes a $\tau\acute{e}\chi\nu\eta$ in full right.[15] It becomes respectable. And the meaning of the word becomes somehow different. Until Aristotle, people studied how to gain approval, by more or less irrational means. But this study, according to Aristotle, is unscientific and has nothing to do with the real $\tau\acute{e}\chi\nu\eta$.[16]

Only the reasoning on which the proof rests can be the object of a really scientific study;[17] and this postulate is the core of his own treatise.

Rhetoric can now become a τέχνη; Aristotle agrees with Plato that it was not one before. He even says in another work, the *Sophistical Refutations* (184a), that Gorgias' activity, which provided easy prescriptions, was quick, but not scientific, ταχεῖα μέν, ἄτεχνος δέ; for people like him started to teach by offering not the τέχνη but only its practical application: οὐ . . . τέχνην, ἀλλὰ τὰ ἀπὸ τῆς τέχνης. This stern distinction explains why he says, in the opening part of the *Rhetoric*, that people have till now practiced rhetoric through chance or habit, but that one may try and understand the causes under-lying their activity—which is the task of a τέχνη.

Thus rhetoric, in this new form, becomes a τέχνη. And it is a very new form indeed. It could not receive the same definition. Could one go on saying that rhetoric produces persuasion, as Plato had said in the *Gorgias*?[18] Aristotle sees quite correctly that this could only be said of the practical teaching of rhetoric; and he answers with a neat new definition: "Its object is not to persuade but to see the possibilities attached to each case, as in all τέχναι" (1355b). Rhetoric has now acquired the safe and unquestionable quality of theoretical knowledge. This is shown by the fact that Aristotle never praises the *logos*, as Gorgias and Isocrates had done; he defends, with more accuracy and more ambition, the science of rhetoric, which is something altogether different.

That rhetoric has now reached this scientific status does not, however, mean it will get mixed up with other forms of scientific reflection. Plato had pretended in the *Phaedrus* that rhetoric, before it became scientific, ought to go all the way round and pass through dialectic itself, and that then, having achieved this glorious knowledge—provided it could—it would lose all point and interest and, so to speak, would melt away like snow when confronted with the bright sunlight of truth. But Aristotle's rhetoric does not have to follow this long and indirect course. He starts from the fact that the art of speech rests on a precise and particular kind of reasoning. Therefore rhetoric, which is the study of this kind of reasoning, has its own subject matter and method. It can stand on its own, in an honorable vicinity. It can be compared with dialectic. This comparison becomes easier because dialectic itself now receives, by contrast, a more precise definition. From Aristotle's works on logic, it emerges that he also considers dialectic from the point of view of method and reasoning. It is no longer a means of reaching absolute truth but a means of discussing any given thesis in a correct manner.

As could be expected, we are thus led to a new classification of τέχναι, or at least to a new pair of τέχναι, where rhetoric finds a new correspondent. Aristotle does not start with a distinction between soul and body; he has too precise a notion of the specific and peculiar nature of each art or science to be so rash or so simple. He does not give a whole system. But he boldly opens the first book of his *Rhetoric* with the statement that rhetoric is parallel, or ἀντίστροφος, to something [19]—not to adorning one's self, as in the *Gorgias*, not to gymnastic, as in the *Antidosis*, but, with the most unexpected, bold, and ambitious choice, precisely to dialectic: Ἡ ῥητορική ἐστιν ἀντίστροφος τῇ διαλεκτικῇ. They share in common the fact of not implying a special field of competence but applying to all cases; one rests on perfect reasoning (with the syllogism), the other on more practical deduction (the enthymeme), but they are exactly parallel. If that is not a complete reversal of Plato's criticism, I wonder what can be.

What an ascent, from the low status of flattery, to intellectual training, and now to what was, for Plato, the highest of all philosophical activities! If polemic is at the root of all these discussions about arts that are ἀντίστροφοι, as seems obvious enough, Aristotle's opening line is the strongest and clearest polemic we have met till now. It could be added that it recurs a few pages later. Aristotle, while discussing the power of rhetoric, starts his sentence with a fresh statement of the same idea: "That rhetoric does not belong to one special field apart from others but, just as dialectic . . .";[20] so no doubt can be left about his clarity or insistence in this new arrangement of disciplines.

Yet I am afraid we cannot just stop there and be content; for things are not so simple. Aristotle's reflection on logic implied, for rhetoric, a number of other connections, which soon make the pattern more complicated.

First, the manner of reasoning—it belongs to logic, but it differs from the perfect and necessary syllogism. And it seems that, after a while, Aristotle came to realize that the whole value of the argument rested on the choice and value of the πρότασις or premise. Thus we are led to the field of δόξα; for there is no radical difference, as Plato had suggested there was, between the methods that aim at truth and those that aim at likelihood, or, as Aristotle says, at "what is similar to truth."[21] Isocrates' modest reliance on δόξα is here, in a way, justified, against Plato. Indeed, Aristotle goes on to say that what is true and just has generally a greater power with men than the reverse and that, whenever it fails to win, this is the orator's fault. The proof itself must, therefore, pass through assumptions commonly entertained, what Aristotle calls τὰ κοινὰ in 1355a27.[22]

If you are going to use such reasoning in practical or political advice, you have to get a clear knowledge of moral and political matters, or passions and characters; that is, you have to deal with ethics and politics. All this analysis is, for Aristotle, a description of premises with which, in order to reason correctly, you have to start. But, as soon as Aristotle has thus broadened his theme and admitted into it the proofs, or πίστεις, founded on the audience's dispositions, he opens the way to something that does not exist in dialectic and that breaks the ἀντίστροφος relation. And that is how we discover, at first to our surprise, but in fact in a very logical way, the existence of a slightly different, and probably later, system.

In 1356a20 ff, rhetoric and dialectic are no longer on the same level, or ἀντίστροφοι; rhetoric is a sort of lateral offspring of dialectic, growing by its side: παραφυές τι, as Aristotle says, using a word found nowhere else in classical Greek. He also says that it is a part of dialectic, which is similar to it: μόριόν τι τῆς διαλεκτικῆς καὶ ὁμοία. Rhetoric seems to have sunk from its former status.

But what it has lost in its relation to dialectic is soon compensated by what it gains elsewhere. All this teaching about προτάσεις connects rhetoric not only with dialectic but with a new science, which Aristotle seems to have been the first to call by its new name, ethics. And ethics is in a way what Plato called politics. This accounts for the manner in which Aristotle's sentence goes on with its new description of rhetoric: παραφυές τι τῆς διαλε-κτικῆς καὶ τῆς περὶ τὰ ἤθη πραγματείας, ἣν δίκαιόν ἐστι προσαγορεύειν πολιτικήν (an offspring of dialectic and of concern with ethics, which is justly called politics).

This arrangement is new and belongs to a more recent part of the *Rhetoric*, according to the different scholars who have studied the composition of that treatise, including Friedrich Solmsen.[23] It is less polemical than the opening statement and much closer to the views of

Plato's *Gorgias*; for it was in the *Gorgias* that Plato gave a general name to the art dealing with the soul, calling it politics. It was also in the *Gorgias* that Plato showed flattery introducing a fake art under the appearance of each genuine one: ὑποδῦσα and ὑπέδυ were used in the *Gorgias* at 464c. Now Aristotle declares in the sentence describing his new arrangement that rhetoric and those who pretend to it "assume the appearance" of politics, whether by ignorance, arrogance, or other human causes (ὑποδύεται ὑπὸ τὸ σχῆμα τῆς πολιτικῆς). The very vocabulary implies an open reference to the *Gorgias*, and Aristotle seems to adopt Plato's views as expressed there.

But, of course, he follows him in order to correct him. Even if rhetoric should never be confused with politics or taken for politics, both of them are still τέχναι. They have different objects, but also something in common. Aristotle expresses a difference, not a condemnation or a dismissal.

Similarly, he seems to be getting nearer to Isocrates, as Isocrates had professed that his rhetoric taught morals and politics,[24] and Aristotle's scheme finally reveals a connection between them. But, here again, there is also a correction. For Aristotle does not say that the practice of rhetoric teaches either virtue or political wisdom; he says just the reverse, namely, that its reasoning rests not on virtue but on some knowledge of the science of ethics, not on political wisdom but on some knowledge about political situations and common opinions in that field—not "teaches," but "rests on."[25] To the end, Aristotle keeps to the idea of τέχνη, which he has succeeded in restoring. Thanks to it, he can discard both Plato's skepticism and Isocrates' naive optimism.

This complicated and subtle image of the relationship between rhetoric and its neighbors is not the last in Greek literature, but it is the last dealt with here.[26] It provides a sort of synthesis, leaving rhetoric in the position of a full-grown τέχνη with respectable companions, including dialectic, ethics, and politics.

To give the picture its finishing touch, I shall only add a word about the two τέχναι previously associated with rhetoric: medicine and gymnastic. The parallel between rhetoric and medicine does not really recur. But, in chapter 1 of his *Rhetoric*, when Aristotle wants to give rhetoric its real scientific function, which is not to persuade but to see the possibilities offered in each case, he uses the simile of medicine (1355b12: οὐδὲ γὰρ ἰατρικῆς . . .).[27] He can use it because, now at last, rhetoric is a τέχνη in the full sense of the word.

On the other hand, gymnastic cannot have anything to do with what Aristotle calls rhetoric. Music, yes. He is happy to adopt Plato's double training for the young: music and gymnastic, one educating the soul and the other the body. But whereas Plato included speech in music (*Republic* 376e), Aristotle, to avoid all ambiguity, in book 8 of the *Politics* treats of music from a purely musical point of view. Both are here practical training. And this treatment offers a sort of confirmation of what we have seen: Isocrates' ambition finally aimed at nothing more than a child's practical exercise.

This is only a detail; but it settles everything in the right place, as is always the case with Aristotle. I have added it for the sheer pleasure of an additional proof, as one might add *quod erat demonstrandum*.

By slight shifts of meaning and precise rectifications, rhetoric has thus passed through a series of steps and moved in a continuous progress, which finally settles it at the highest place among authentic sciences. It is no longer Gorgias' rhetoric, not by far. It has gained in lucidity. But it remains for us to see what it has lost thereby and what was the practical result of this promotion toward reason and austerity. The magic of speech, the magic of style, no longer had a place in the new rhetoric. The defense of rhetoric as a τέχνη had meant a divorce from its seductive and attractive marvels. Could this magic come back? Could new tendencies restore its glamour? The new trend had been so powerful that any effort in that direction could only be long and hard. That is why the next chapter, which will be devoted to this problem, will take us quite a distance away from the fourth century. It takes time to free one's self from the combined authority of Plato, Isocrates, and Aristotle.

IV

Logic versus Magic:
Aristotle and Later Writers

IV The authors of the fourth century B.C., as we have seen, had broken all connection between magic and rhetoric; our task now will be to try and see whether this connection could ever be re-established. But we must first answer a question, which indeed the very title of these lectures calls for: Exactly what was the meaning of such a connection? It was, no doubt, no more than a simile; but this simile had some significance, and it is time for us to make it clearer.

It can be traced, I think, on different levels. If we adhere to what Gorgias had said, his simile may lead to two different attitudes concerning literature and style. He believed that speech, like inspired poetry, had an irrational power and impact of its own. Persuasion, in that case, rests not only on proof but on suggestion, style, and emotion. Although Gorgias wanted to create a τέχνη, he took such means into account and thought they were of primary importance. This belief, in turn, may lead to a special taste in style, which insists on the poetical, on the strange, on the refined. Such had been Gorgias' style.

But if we look at what existed before Gorgias, we must remember that poetry had first been inspired and that magic had been divine. Authors could claim that they practiced something more than just a τέχνη and confess to an irrational impulse. Gorgias, so far as we know, had not put forward any such claim. But it could be done, as can be seen in some half-serious examples, such as Socrates' first speech in the *Phaedrus*.

This irrational impulse could also have something to do with actual magic. Of course, one can love style and admire the power of speech without believing in witch-craft—luckily enough! But the fact remains that such a view of oratory reckons with the irrational. The more one insists on it, the more one may be prone to acknowl-edge irrational powers in other fields as well. When one begins with the irrational, it is hard to know where to stop. Gorgias, so far as we know, had not followed that line at all, but other authors could be fascinated by occultism as well as by the glamour of inspiration.

However, the theorists of the fourth century had equally refused all the different meanings this simile could involve: they had disregarded the irrational impact of oratory, the poetical strangeness in style, and any reliance on inspiration. They had made a choice.

In order to get a clearer view of what was at stake in such a choice, we shall now draw a contrast: we shall first try and see how far Aristotle had actually gone in that direction and then how, in the course of centuries, people eventually tried, with varying success, to find some remedy, φάρμακον, against this overintellectual approach.

Aristotle's treatment of rhetoric was, in a way, negative; for, with him, most of the traditional parts of rhetoric were gradually absorbed by logic and thereby lost their importance. The very structure of Aristotle's *Rhetoric* offers a clear proof of this fact. Naturally, in his effort to transform rhetoric into a τέχνη, he was bound to leave out all that was outside the τέχνη, or, as he says, ἄτεχνον, "extratechnic," "untechnical." Thus he first blames previous authors for having dealt only with what is not proof and therefore is just appendage (1354a14: προσθῆκαι). By that he means, as the context clearly explains, all that does not bear on the matter but is directed toward the judge in order to rouse his emotions. That was Gorgias' main interest; it now drops away, leaving us with the proof as the core of rhetoric.

But, in the second section of the same book 1, we learn that there are two kinds of proofs. One of them has nothing to do with τέχνη: all questions of fact, testimonies, confessions, and the like. These Aristotle says he will only mention in cursory fashion (ἐπιδραμεῖν, 1375a23) in the last chapter of book 1, as belonging to judicial eloquence. Something else, then, drops away.

We are thus left with the three kinds of "technical" proofs, which rest on the character of the speaker, the passion of the audience, and the demonstration proper. But, although all three are present, it is only fair to observe that they do not have equal importance, from either a practical or an intellectual point of view. Logical demonstration is treated in book 1 §§3–15, then again in book 2 §§18–26. Aristotle begins with it and ends with it.[1] This treatment, by itself, means giving it pride of place. But, more noticeable still, the demonstration proper commands the whole analysis. The discussion of ἤθη and πάθη, which comes in between, is not what another author would have meant it to be; its real point is to provide προτάσεις, or basic assumptions, in the argumentation. It is therefore subordinated to the demonstration from the very start.

Also, from this discussion of ἤθη and πάθη, Aristotle draws conclusions about the arguments that are likely to produce the right reaction in the audience. What could be more distant from magic than such means? Let us quote his conclusion in the case of anger, for instance: "We have explained against whom one feels anger, and in which disposition, and for what causes; it is clear that the speaker should put his audience into these dispositions and show that the other party has the behavior and character that call for anger" (1380a1–4). This conclusion is logical enough, but it obviously cannot be of any practical use. It gives the theoretical explanation, not the means, of succeeding. And, the word τέχνη having undergone an important shift in meaning, the old aim of producing emotions is commented upon, in a theoretical way, rather than made available for actual use.² One could say that the old pursuit of practical efficacy is one more thing that, more or less, drops away.

Yet there is one feature of speech that cannot so easily be reduced to reasoning or treated from a logical point of view: this feature, which was so capital for Gorgias, is style. And Aristotle did write about style. Book 3 of the *Rhetoric* treats λέξις and τάξις, style and composition. Although there used to be some doubts about its authenticity, they cannot reasonably be entertained any longer. The only remark suggested by the very discussion itself is that the themes of this last book do not belong exactly to the same intellectual process or the same trend of thought as those of the other two. Some scholars are still of opinion that book 3 may have been written at a different time. It is, no doubt, less essential to Aristotle's approach.

What does he say about style? First, he does away with declamation itself (ὑπόκρισις), including voice, gestures, and the like: there is no τέχνη about such things, and they amount only to a regrettable necessity³—another thing drops away (and it could have been magical).

As for style proper, its art has only recently emerged (1403b36). However, Aristotle sketches a short history of style, which is a direct attack on Gorgias. He says style started with poets and that the first prose style was poetical, as was Gorgias' style (1404a26: οἷον ἡ Γοργίου); "and even now," he says, "uncultivated people think that this is a beautiful style. But it is not, and prose style is not poetical style." So farewell to Gorgias' high ambitions! Furthermore, Aristotle's argument is a very sad one: even in poetry, authors have abandoned high style and stopped using words that are not everyday words. He then decides not to mention poetical style, which is treated in the *Poetics*, but only pedestrian style,[4] the great virtue of which is clarity (to be σαφῆ).

Magic is thus brushed away; it can have no place in a style that aims only, or mainly, at clarity.[5] It must be added that this position, so firmly adopted in the very first approach, runs all through Aristotle's analysis of style. He attacks all the devices intended to stir admiration and considers them out of place in prose (1404b); he recommends commonplace words; he criticizes the use of compound words. And the standard that he always upholds as decisive is propriety, or τὸ πρέπον (1404b4, 5, 16, 18, 31; 1405a12, 14; 1406a12, 13, 32; 1406b6; 1408a10; 1414a25, 28); it is also the title of one of the sections (§7).[6] That is to say, he rejects surprise and figures. The style that he recommends should be transparent, not magical.

In the part about style, Gorgias is repeatedly quoted, always as an example of what should not be done.[7] One should not use poetical style, as he does (1404a26), or many compound words, as he does (1405b38), or obscure or surprising meaphors, as he does (1406b9 and 16). We cannot be surprised; we knew that Gorgias had, much earlier, lost the battle of style, at least for a while. Isocrates had been the first to correct him. And, although we cannot judge of Aristotle's own style in his popular works, which are lost, it seems that its qualities were on the whole those that he praises, not poetical glamour. Plato, who wrote against poetry, could use the magic of words and poetic style; Aristotle either could not or would not.[8]

Of course, it may be suggested that, with him, all the magic of style is left to the poets; for he often says in the *Rhetoric* that what is not good in prose may be excellent in verse. But do we find it in the *Poetics*? Alas! Let us read the first sentence about style (λέξις): "The parts of λέξις as a whole are the letter, the syllable, the conjunction, the article, the noun, and the verb." That does not prepare us much for the magic of style. And the virtue of style in poetry? It is not mere clarity, but almost: "The virtue of λέξις is to be clear without being mean" (σαφῆ καὶ μὴ ταπεινήν)⁹—a rather negative statement. Gorgias had wanted prose to be as powerful as poetry; Aristotle would like poetry to be almost as neat as prose. In fact, it has been noticed that in his whole *Poetics* Aristotle does not mention or quote one single instance of lyric verse.¹⁰

Finally, we could mention that Aristotle, although he never uses the concept of ψυχαγωγία in connection with rhetoric, does use it twice for tragedy, but only in the loose meaning of "being impressive": peripeties and recognition scenes, he says, are among the means that most impress people (1450a33: οἷς μάλιστα ψυχαγωγεῖ ἡ τραγῳδία), and the visual aspect itself¹¹ is impressive but does not rest on tragic τέχνη (1450b17: ἡ δὲ ὄψις ψυχαγωγικὸν μέν, ἀτεχνότατον δὲ καὶ ἥκιστα οἰκεῖον τῆς ποιητικῆς). Ψυχαγωγία, therefore, has been not only reduced but, in the last instance, made contemptible.¹²

Yet even in the *Rhetoric*—even there—Aristotle cannot completely do away with high style. For one thing, he had certainly read, or heard, Demosthenes. And he acknowledges that, when people speak παθητικῶς, emotionally compound words, periphrases, and unusual words are fitting (1408b11: ἁρμόττει). Such a style is appropriate when the speaker is in anger or when he compels his audience and raises its emotions through praise, blame, anger, or friendship. And quoting—unfortunately, the example is more timid than the idea¹³—some passages of Isocrates with homoeoteleuton or poetical words, he remarks: "Thus do people speak when possessed (ἐνθουσιάζοντες), and listeners accept it because

they are in a similar state. This is why it is appropriate in poetry; for poetry is inspired" (ἔνθεον).

This loophole, as Fritz Wehrli has seen,[14] is the only
one through which high style and inspiration might come
back. But would they? And could they? Against this
closely locked system, we now have to see whether any
attempt was made to restore some of the old magic.

To follow the evolution of rhetoric and the continued
discussions that it raised after Aristotle—among his
disciples and in Greek or Latin writers, including Cicero,
Quintilian, and others—would need more time and more
knowledge than I actually have. I am not writing a
history of rhetoric; I have not even mentioned important
works that we still possess, such as the *Rhetoric to
Alexander*. Such histories have been written, and very
well written—for instance, by Eduard Norden and,
more recently, by George Kennedy.[15] For our problem,
it seems fairly obvious that all the main theories after
Aristotle can be traced back either to him or to Isocrates,
more generally to both.

Yet there had also been a living tradition of real
oratory, where high style, inspiration, and poetical
diction still reappeared in various ways. Demosthenes
used them in the fourth century. And Hegesias, con-
sciously trying to launch a new fashion, used them with
less restraint, and also less success, in the third century.[16]
In this first appearance of Asianism, one could easily
read a first answer to both Isocrates' and Aristotle's taste.
Still, you will allow me to pass over such examples; for
in order to get a clearer picture I should like to choose a
later period—the first and second centuries A.D.—which
offers a clear-cut contrast with Aristotle's intellectualism.
For there we again find, together with the fashion of
poetical style and the publication of new works on

rhetoric, a remarkable and well-established connection with magic proper.

There is no doubt that this period saw a revival of magic, and, to return to our former distinction, of sacred magic. It was no longer the magic of the γόης; such a word now applied to conjurers and deceivers,[17] who were an object of scorn and prosecution.[18] But the magic of the μάγος and of the sacred healer, the Pythagorean magic, was then again in full bloom. The life of Apollonius of Tyana shows that it existed: Apollonius could heal people, he had visions, he could foretell the future. He was a Pythagorean, obeying all the rules of life of the old master, and he had been in close relation with the μάγοι. He was considered as using τῇ μάγῳ τέχνῃ. In fact, he was accused of being a γόης and had to defend himself against the accusation; Philostratus reproduces a very long speech of his, in which he clears himself, drawing a contrast between wisdom and wizardry,[19] or religion and wizardry (8.7). Philostratus himself insists, with a sort of passion, that Apollonius prophesied not by being a γόης but by divine inspiration (5.12, 7.39)—which so resembles the sacred magic of yore that Apollonius was considered a new incarnation of Proteus.

Apollonius was no rhetorician or orator; but his life suggests the atmosphere. Also, he was not an isolated case. The name of Alexander, the fake prophet (ψευδόμαντις), has been made famous by Lucian; and we know that this Alexander, who forged a new divinity and new oracles, had received lessons from one of Apollonius' friends and that he claimed to resemble Pythagoras. Even among sophists and rhetoricians we find several people accused of practicing magic. Glen Bowersock in his *Greek Sophists in the Roman Empire* recalls the accusations against Dionysius of Miletus, who was supposed to have trained his disciples in rhetoric through the use of magic, or of Hadrian of Tyre, who, when he died, was believed to be a magician.[20] Such accusations remind us of the case of Apuleius. But there was also sacred magic, particularly the magic cures of Asclepius, about which Professor Bowersock remarks that "the second century saw a simultaneous resurgence of both rational and irrational healing."[21] The sophist Aristides was an adept in such sacred magic.

In that new atmosphere we also find a new trend among some of the theorists who speak about style and rhetoric, and a new literary taste among the so-called sophists. The reaction of the former is more timid, that of the latter more drastic, but in both we can detect a longing for things that Aristotle had cast away. In the case of the theorists, this new trend can be illustrated by two authors: the author of the treatise *On the Sublime*, who wrote in the first century, and Aristides, who wrote in the second.

The treatise *On the Sublime* is still very modest. All the same, the author believes that rhetoric should aim at something higher than just reason and clarity, as is suggested by the very title. He provides testimony that a new trend exists in oratory; for he speaks of a search for originality (5)[22] and of orators who see the Erinyes, as tragic poets would (15.8). He is against such excess, since he thinks sublimity should arise mainly from nobility of ideas and ideals. But that means that he believes in sublimity itself, and he has a very acute feeling for its power—not the power of speech as such, but the power of a particular kind of speech. When he writes about it, he becomes very eloquent indeed. He says that sublime speech "does not produce persuasion in the audience, but enchantment and ecstasy (ἔκστασιν); it also startles (σὺν ἐκπλήξει) and thus acquires an influence and power that is irresistible" (δυναστείαν καὶ βίαν ἄμαχον). Indeed, when it appears, "it scatters everything away like thunder" (1.4–5). He repeats later that it is hard, nay, impossible to resist the sublime (7.3: δύσκολος δέ, μᾶλλον δ᾽ ἀδύνατος ἡ κατεξανάστασις). He even remarks that a noble emotion, coming in at the right time, breathes with enthusiasm as if under the sway of madness and inspiration and, in a way, inspires the speaker (8.4: οἱονεὶ φοιβάζον τοὺς λόγους).

Still more remarkably, he admits the power of sheer harmony. Here again we come very close to the old magical notion; for he says that flute playing inspires emotions (πάθη) and carries away lucid judgment in a sort of possession, making people ἔκφρονας καὶ κορυβαντι-ασμοῦ πλήρεις (39.2). He recalls that there is a spell, θέλγητρον, in lyre playing. Word arrangement can, he thinks, produce a similar effect, for it has a magic charm (39.3: κηλεῖν); he even declares that everybody knows this by common experience! No doubt all this implies a very different kind of eloquence from what we have seen with Isocrates and Aristotle. Our author has a feeling for style. He likes Demosthenes more than Lysias or Isocrates; he even quotes Thucydides and the poets. And he believes in some sort of inspiration.[23] It is almost the magic of style.

Why not quite? Because, although he has such feelings, he thinks that there is a τέχνη of this sublimity;[24] and, when he tries to find out its rules and say how one must write or how not, good taste again prevails. Rhetoric is not poetry; figures, metaphors, and the like are excellent for the sublime—oh, so excellent!—but provided they are neither too numerous nor out of place. And that is why people laugh at Gorgias for calling Xerxes the Persian Zeus (3.2) or using similar expressions. Therefore the treatise is more interesting for the sort of longing it

displays for high style and the magic of speech than for
the doctrine it presents. Otherwise, Boileau obviously
could not have chosen to translate it into French.

Aristides' discussion of rhetoric is not much more
audacious, but it moves in the same direction; and,
although the man was still an Atticist, his reaction against
Plato's or Aristotle's austerity is very firm. Aelius
Aristides, six centuries after the *Gorgias*, is still brimming
with indignation against Plato's severity, as if it were a
personal and recent insult. Against Plato, he claims
vigorously that rhetoric is a τέχνη, and a most useful and
noble one. The main part of the first treatise is quite in
line with Isocrates; for he ascertains that rhetoric implies
both serious thinking and the defense of justice, as
opposed to violent action: it protects the weak against
the stronger, since it allows them to be heard, and is the
source of all laws. Indeed rhetoric covers, as its proper
field, laws, justice, and speeches. This is, on the whole,
what Isocrates had said with less polemical insistence.
And, like Isocrates, Aristides feels offended at the low
rank given by Plato to rhetoric; he not only restores its
importance, like Isocrates, by comparing it with gymnastic, but adds the old and, to Plato, scandalous simile
connecting rhetoric and medicine. He compares rhetoric
with both arts[25] and, toward the end, repeats with
increasing energy that rhetoric, being related to the four
virtues, is no flattery; "on the contrary, what both
gymnastic and medicine do for the body—that is, both
taken together—this rhetoric obviously does for the soul
and for political life."[26]

The second speech takes up the same ideas, showing,
against Plato, that the great statesmen did have a good
influence in teaching the people. They did not always
succeed, but neither do the gods. Homer and Hesiod
respected the wise orator; and this proves that rhetoric

is accessory to the art of commanding (σύνεδρος τῆς βασιλικῆς). Indeed, closely imitating the myth of the *Protagoras*, which Isocrates seems to have had in mind when he praised the *logos*, Aristides presents Hermes as sent by Zeus to offer mankind not αἰδώς and δίκη, as in the *Protagoras*, or even the *logos*, as in Isocrates, but rhetoric. It is rhetoric that enables men to found cities and maintain them; it still does in modern times (100–101).

This is being more Isocratean than Isocrates himself. And Aristides' very insistence almost approaches Gorgias' wonder and excitement over the *logos*. It does not, however, return to his ideas, in so far as the author (like Isocrates) refuses to separate rhetoric from wisdom. His position may be compared with Cicero's, in the famous praise of oratory in *De Oratore* 1.30–34; Cicero repeats some of Isocrates' arguments but begins with a personal celebration of the joy of holding people's attention and stirring their emotions at will.

But it must be added that the first part of Aelius Aristides' treatise is not quite so rational as the second. To the reproach that rhetoric is no τέχνη, he there gives a first answer, saying that what comes from the gods is no τέχνη either but is greater than τέχνη (10). He goes on about Delphi and its inspired priestess. He even adds the religious cures at Delphi, which surpass the powers of humble medicine, Delphi's help in the production of political constitutions, and all the wonders of human life that do not rest on τέχνη or knowledge. What if this should be true of rhetoric? After all, he says, poets are praised for what they write without τέχνη; and madness, which is god-sent, is superior to human wisdom.

Here indeed is an opening toward another world. Aelius Aristides loved all the lowest forms of religion.[27] He wrote several works about the sacred cures he had himself experienced thanks to Asclepius, about his dreams, about prophecies and omens of all sorts. He could well believe in some kind of inspired oratory. Did he not declare, in his treatise Περὶ τοῦ παραφθέγματος, p. 369: "We too declare that what we say comes from the Muses and the gods" (as do Hesiod and Pindar)? Did he not use in another speech the Orpheus simile, in order to judge of the power of lack of power of orators? What causes success in the practice of oratory is not flattery but the inspiration that god gives to those who deserve it; if orators were τέλεοι τὴν μουσικὴν, accomplished in music, "and if they had all that Orpheus is reported to have had, they would be followed by all people." [28]

Such sentences take us very far not only from Plato and Aristotle but from Isocrates, and they remind us of what had caused Gorgias' wonder. Yet they are but isolated sentences. On the whole, Aristides has not overcome the intellectual trend of the fourth century. He mentions this inspired oratory in the beginning of his treatise, but, in what follows, he defends rhetoric from the point of view of τέχνη. And if he had a glimpse of the inspired style, he certainly did not practice it himself. Philostratus never tried to praise him for such qualities. [29]

From these examples, it seems to emerge that theorists felt that something had been lost, but remained very shy in trying to recapture it. Yet, if we read Philostratus' *Lives of the Sophists*, it becomes obvious that the movement of the second sophistic as a whole was making progress in that direction. For suddenly the picture changes, and magical rhetoric returns.

Professor Bowersock will not, I hope, resent my considering once more the second sophistic from the point of view of style and literature; "It could be argued without apology," he wrote, "that the Second Sophistic has more importance in Roman History than it has in Greek Literature."[30] This may well be true if we consider its achievements; yet it presented a number of features that seem to me to be of interest, if not for Greek literature, at least for my own limited theme.

The second sophistic was a product of Asia. Aristides, although an Atticist and not an Asianist, was born in Mysia. All the great sophists lived in cities like Smyrna or Ephesus,[31] and most of them were born in Asia. Nicetes came from Smyrna, Isaeus from Assyria, Dionyius from Miletus, Lollianus from Ephesus, Polemo from Laodicea, Antiochus and Alexander Peloplato from Cilicia, Hadrian and Maximus from Tyre; and the list could be much longer. The new trend in rhetoric was not invented in Greece proper; its adherents brought new blood from abroad, just as Gorgias, coming from Sicily, had done.

As we have seen Aelius Aristides answering Plato's *Gorgias* in theoretical discussion, so we see our sophists actually praising Gorgias himself and considering him again as the great man. Philostratus starts with him; he is the father of the art of the sophists, he says (p. 208, §492). And in the course of his work he often mentions Gorgias' influence on several of the sophists, as he does for Scopelian,[32] less explicitly for Hadrian of Tyre,[33] but again for Proclus of Naucratis.[34] He also uses the word γοργιάζειν (Gorgianize) several times.[35] The very title "second sophistic" may owe its origin to such a reappraisal.

And it is our Gorgias, as we have tried to describe him. In fact, Philostratus insists on the idea that Gorgias used the same devices as Aeschylus, achieving the same overwhelming greatness, and using poetical words to enhance the majesty of his style. But then, Philostratus also presents this influence of poetry as one of the main features of the second sophistic. Hadrian of Tyre was inspired by tragedy.[36] Nicagoras used to say that tragedy was the mother of the art of the sophists; and Hippodromus added that Homer, in that case, was the father.[37]

Such statements already imply a reaction in taste and style. In Philostratus, the different sophists are often praised for their voice and acting, for their rhythm or harmony, for their power; the irrational part in oratory has recovered its importance. This is apparent in the very subjects of the new orators. They loved, as Gorgias had, official speeches, such as panegyrics or funeral orations. They also liked to give a touch of the poetical by calling some of them songs, ᾠδαὶ or μονῳδίαι or παλινῳδίαι.[38] Their effect on the audience is often one of exalted marveling too: people listened to Hadrian of Tyre as to a nightingale and rushed to hear him (p. 256, §589). People listened to Polemo with increasing wonder and admiration (p. 230, §538). Sometimes this effect is even described in the words or metaphors of poetical magic and is projected back into the past; for who would have believed that the wise Isocrates would get, for his funeral monument, a singing Siren?[39] Yet Philostratus is happy to convey that information (p. 213, §503). And Prodicus? He also becomes endowed with irrational powers; and he is said to have cast a spell over his listeners (θέλγων) in the manner of Orpheus or Thamyris (p. 203, §483). But then, in the second sophistic, this is also true of Scopelian; we see him chosen as an ambassador because the affairs needed a speaker who could cast a spell over people (θέλξειν) in the manner of Orpheus and Thamyris.[40] As for Polydeuces—whose eloquence is described by two quotations, one of which is a praise of Proteus for his power of transformation—he is said to have "charmed" the king with his voice (p. 258, §593: θέλξας).

How did they succeed in having such influence? Not by magic, of course (although some of them were accused of being conjurers); but, although they learned, used, and taught τέχνη, and although Philostratus is always careful to explain who had been each sophist's master, there is some touch of the inspired about many of them.

First, Philostratus accepts a magical tradition as regards the first sophistic: Protagoras had had contact with the Persian μάγοι (p. 210, §494). Then he hints at similar characteristics in some of the sophists of the second sophistic: Hadrian of Tyre was held a magician because he talked marvels about the μάγοι (p. 210, §494); and Polemo spoke "as from the tripod" (p. 232, §542), not to mention the "frenzied" Nicetes (p. 217, §511: ὑπόβακχος). That such a view of oratory often lent a warm and passionate character to the very style of these authors was natural enough, and Philostratus often remarks on the fact in his appreciation of the sophists.[41] Now, we have no reason here to start a discussion about style. But the whole collection of testimonials suggests a deliberate attempt to infuse some new and free strength in oratory by returning to the old alliance, first embodied in Gorgias, between magic and rhetoric. With a revival of the irrational in life and thought came a revival in the attempt to restore to speech its irrational impact and power.

As could easily be guessed in advance, this new impulse showed most clearly not in the theoretical analysis of people who tried to delineate the rules of a τέχνη but in a work like Philostratus' *Lives of the Sophists*, which was by no means a τέχνη but a work of literary criticism dealing with the actual attitude and success of orators.

But the attempt was artificial. It did not produce a new style, nor did it produce much new thought. It is interesting mainly because it shows that, beside the elegant purity at which Atticism was still aiming, this short-lived Asianism reveals, in the full light of history, an obstinate longing toward something that had been lost for several centuries under the weight of overintellectual methods.

The struggle between these two trends could, of course, be followed not only in Greek and Latin prose—where Norden has traced it with much insight and clarity—but in all literatures and at all times. After all, it amounts to a struggle between the spell of the irrational and the desire to master it by means of reason, which were precisely the two aims Gorgias had tried to combine and conciliate. But, through all these alternate movements between one tendency and the other, no one ever tried to reach, in fact, the pre-Gorgian condition and count only on magic and on inspiration. No one, at least, until our present time, which could be described as the exact reverse of Aristotle's rationalism.

First came the magic of words. This we find everywhere from the symbolist movement onward. It started, naturally enough, with poetry; and it was again and again maintained that poetry rests on this magic spell. Baudelaire wrote somewhere that to use a language well was to practice a sort of magic: "une espèce de sorcellerie évocatoire." Mallarmé went further, speaking of the sorcery that belongs to poetry ("le sortilège que restera la poésie") and saying that anyone able to coin a verse where usual expressions would meet so as to form a new word, foreign to the actual language, had reached something like incantation ("un mot total, neuf, étranger à la langue, et comme incantatoire"). This magical quality was a cause for wonder among surrealist writers. André Breton gave voice to the feeling when he called Baudelaire "the first seer, the king of poets, a real god."[42]

Where could this magic come from? Not, of course, from τέχνη, not from divine inspiration either, but from that most irrational of all sources: from an inward inspiration arising out of the unconscious self, in some sort of spontaneous language obeying this mysterious inspiration.[43] Hence the experiences of automatic writing and what Breton called "magic dictation."[44] That these were, once more, connected with a deep regard for occultism is certain. One of his works is called "Entrée des Mediums"; and one of the best critics wrote that his work was much indebted to a sort of parapsychologic spiritism, "a distant heir of Orphism and Neoplatonic mysteries."[45] And there, in the mystery of irrational language, arose once again several of the ancient magical habits relished so much by Gorgias: spontaneous puns, sounds conveying, in a half-serious game, a sort of magic meaning. Herodicus, the ancient Pythagorean, used to say that Thrasymachus was bold in fighting (θρασυ-μάχαις); Breton felt moved by the idea that Pierre Reverdy was the stone that actually does become green: "la pierre qui amasse mousse."[46]

Such habits look like esoteric research within a small group of people. But something quite different has turned out to be the case. If we consider contemporary literature, at least in France, we cannot doubt that it has become irrational, illogical, startling. Novels do not follow any chronological or logical order. They adore puns of all sorts and marvel at their symbolic value. They love long, unfinished sentences, which develop like incomplete revelations of some truth that will by nature always remain out of reach. Writing has become a sacred and mysterious operation; words themselves seem to haunt the writer, like magic formulas coming from nowhere. Ultimately, people say that language itself is the real speaker.[47] Both the author and his subject matter are, so to speak, absorbed by its irrational domination.

One might expect that rhetoric, conversely, would fall under heavy condemnation. But the remarkable thing is that it has not. As soon as language itself seemed to command all forms of expression, a new rhetoric came into being. Linguistic theories helped it to grow and take shape.[48] And this new rhetoric shows features taken from Aristotle. A ready example is Roland Barthes' commentary on Balzac's short story called "Sarrasine." There, he speaks of topic, of proairesis, of proof and syllogism, even of enthymeme.[49] But he refuses to read a text as a logical sequence offering one single meaning; he looks for a plurality of meanings, for connotations and symbols. Classical rhetoric is treated as obsolete. It is as obsolete as faith in the very transparence and objectivity of language.

This sketch, of course, gives an oversimplified view of a phenomenon that is both general and varied. It also ignores the different schools in linguistics or literary criticism, and their discussions, which are often quite passionate. But these very discussions prove that, in a way, the open trial of logic versus magic is still being debated, as it was in antiquity, but with a complete reversal in the chances of each party. I mention the fact as a sort of appendix to my present theme, because it shows that the most formal discussions in ancient Greece —for what could seem more formal, nay, artificial and devoid of connection with our own life than the problem of rhetoric?—still have their value for us and their bearing on our problems. In a time when we have so many texts about speech and language and when the problem of speech has become so prominent, reflection on rhetoric and its rational or irrational nature does concern us. It may even help us. I have been candid in showing the shortcomings that could result, from an artistic point of view, from the rationalistic attitude of the fourth century B.C. But is it necessary to point out that the reverse attitude is at least as dangerous, that the cult of the irrational in its various forms may well threaten not only our literature but our social and political life? The pendulum oscillates from one excess to the other. Returning to the authors of the fifth century B.C. means returning to a time when things were not yet separated and isolated, when rationalism and irrational habits, μῦθος and *logos*, inspiration and τέχνη, went hand in hand. Returning to the fifth century B.C. means recapturing that wonderful collaboration of opposites. Were I English, I should say in conclusion, "Perhaps we could do worse." Since I am French, you will allow me to declare, "Surely we could not do better."

Notes

Index

Notes

I. Gorgias and Magic

1. See below, n. 7.
2. *Harvard Studies in Classical Philology* 66 (1962) 99–155.
3. *Journal of Hellenic Studies* 93 (1973) 155–162.
4. *Od.* 12.41: θέλγουσιν. Although much is said about the pleasure of poetry, the word θελκτήριον is used only once in connection with it (*Od.* 1.337).
5. *Nem.* 4.3, 8.48; *Pyth.* 3.64.
6. Plutarch *Mor.* 348c.
7. Gorgias speaks of ἀλλοτρίων τε πραγμάτων καὶ σωμάτων (9). Several centuries later Iamblichus still uses, in his description of catharsis in tragedy, the notion of ἀλλότρια πάθη (*De Myst.* 1.11, pp. 40–41 Bithel). Cf. W. Süss, *Ethos* (Leipzig, 1910), p. 93.
8. *Il.* 23.108, 153; 24.507; *Od.* 4.113, 183; 19.249.
9. Aristotle *Poetics* 1449b27; see also 1452b36 and 1453b1. The exact nature of these two emotions has been discussed by W. Schadewaldt, "Furcht und Mitleid?," *Hermes* 83 (1955) 129–171 (*Hellas und Hesperien*, Zurich and Stuttgart, 1960, pp. 346–388), and M. Pohlenz, "Furcht and Mitleid, Ein Nachwort," *Hermes* 84 (1956) 49–74. The result of the discussion could be said to have made somewhat clearer the strong and irrational character these emotions have—which fits in well with Gorgias. The importance of the physical manifestations they produce and their relation to medicine has been emphasized by H. Flashar, "Das Lehre von der Wirkung der Dichtung in der griechischen Poetik," *Hermes* 84 (1956) 12–48; but this notion should not be pressed too far. What Gorgias really has in mind is emotion as a means of modifying people's opinions.
10. Pleasure and pain recur in the philosophers; see Plato *Rep.* 413b (where fear is added and the word γοητευθέντες is used), Aristotle *Rhet.* 1378a20 (where anger, pity, and fear are added).
11. *Phaedrus* 267c, Hermias ad loc. = fr. B6 DK. Hermias uses both οἶκτον and ἔλεον.
12. See also *Rhet.* 1419b ff. Cicero's praise of speech, *De Oratore* 1.53, keeps to Gorgias' tradition, but with a list more simple and more adapted to everyday practice; he speaks of exciting anger,

hate, and sorrow, or calming these emotions and producing kindness and pity.

13. When Protagoras, in Plato's dialogue bearing his name, says that the poets and seers were the first sophists (316d), that is a slightly different idea; what he means is that they were educators, as were the sophists. Yet this is one more link between two literary activities that, for us, seem very remote from each other.

14. The meaning of the expression is complex; for *poiesis* is creation, and art, not only poetry. Poetical prose may be simply prose that is artfully managed and organized, but literary prose was invented in order to emulate the dignity of poetry.

15. Cf. Aristotle in Quintil. 3.1.13, Cicero *Orator* 176. See also Dionys. *De Isocr.* 1.

16. In [Dem.] *Erot.* 2, we also read that solemn speeches should be composed ποιητικῶς καὶ περιττῶς. On the other hand, Alcidamas protests with an opposition between the ῥήτωρ δεινός and the ποιητής λόγων ἱκανός (*Soph.* 12).

17. He may have used rhythm before Gorgias, since he was already well known in 427 (cf. Aristophanes *Banqueters*, fr. 168 K), and his name remained attached to it (see Cicero *Orator* 175); yet what we can judge of his style in a late period suggests prudence.

18. See, for Thrasymachus, F. Blass, *Die attische Beredsamkeit*, II, 2nd ed. (Leipzig, 1892), p. 155. For Gorgias, this new habit appears more clearly in the *Palamedes* than in his other works; *ibid.*, p. 141.

19. At *Panathenaicus* 2, Isocrates connects the kind of speeches he has decided to write with the Panhellenic tradition (which can be traced back to Gorgias) and speaks of them as πολλῶν μὲν ἐνθυμημάτων γέμοντας, οὐκ ὀλίγων δ' ἀντιθέσεων καὶ παρισώσεων καὶ τῶν ἄλλων ἰδεῶν which compel the audience to display loud approval. This description would surely fit Gorgias' style, and antithesis comes before all other figures.

20. *HSCP* 50 (1939) 35–84, reprinted in *Three Essays on Thucydides* (Cambridge, Mass., 1967), pp. 55–117.

21. *Der Einfluss der gr. Poesie auf Gorgias, der Begründer der att. Kunstprosa* (Munich-Würzburg, 1907–1909). Cf. p. 57: "So ergibt sich mit Notwendigkeit die Folgerung dass Gorgias seine rhetorischen Figuren von der Poesie übernahm." See also G. Kennedy, *The Art of Persuasion in Greece* (Princeton, 1963), p. 33, where he traces the use of antithesis in Hesiod, Theognis, and other poets.

22. See Thrasymachus fr. 1 DK, lines 6 ff, or fr. 2: Ἀρχελάῳ δουλεύσομεν Ἕλληνες ὄντες βαρβάρῳ;

23. Another quotation of his works is for using tragic diction in an ironical manner (1406b16: ἄριστα τῶν τραγικῶν, cf. 1408b20).

24. I should like to refer here to A. Barb's brilliant paper "The Survival of Magic Arts," *The Conflict between Paganism and Christianity in the Fourth Century*, Essays ed. by A. Momigliano (Oxford, 1963), pp. 100–125.

25. See below, p. 27.

26. See the discussion in P. Boyancé, *Le culte des Muses chez les philosophes grecs* (Paris, 1937), particularly p. 31.

27. In tragedy there seems to be a separation between inspired or magic utterances on the one hand and poetical expression on the other; but the effects of both can still be combined.

28. See below, n. 50.

29. See, for the ἀρά, *Septem* 70, 645, 655, 709, 723, 766, 785, 787, 831–833, 840, 954; *Agamemnon* 457, 1409, 1413, 1601; *Choephori* 406, 692, 912; *Eumenides* 417.

30. In Lucian, going alive to the nether world replaces calling the dead into ours.

31. See *Od.* 11.34: εὐχωλῇσι λιτῇσί τε, and in Lucian, 7: ῥῆσίν τινα μακρὰν . . . τὴν ἐπῳδήν . . . τὴν ἐπῳδὴν ἐκείνην. For other examples of νεκυομαντεία see Herodotus 5.92 and other passages and, for magic proper, *Pap. Mag. Lond.* 121.285.

32. See *Pap. Mag. Lond.* 121.299 or 46.321 and 326; also *Pap. Mag. Par.* 1.2176. The verb is coupled with γοητεῦσαι in Dio Chrys. 50.5. And Plato (*Laws* 933a) speaks of magical action obtained through μαγγανείαις τέ τισιν καὶ ἐπῳδαῖς καὶ καταδέσεσι λεγομέναις.

33. *On the Sacred Disease* 1–2. It may be added, as a counterpart, that there were drugs against madness and psychological troubles; see P. M. Schuhl, in *Annales Moreau de Tours*, III (Paris, 1967), p. 70. As is well known, Helen (*Od.* 4.221) uses a drug that can calm sorrow and anger; the Greeks were quite aware of the interaction between soul and body.

34. See Gorgias, A2 and 10 DK.

35. Rostagni gives good reason to retain the story as authentic (in *Studi it. fil. class.* 2:1–147, arguing against Diels, *Sitzb. Berl. Ak. phil.-hist.*, 1884, I, p. 344). The source is Satyrus, in Diogenes Laert. 8.59.

36. Empedocles is occasionally connected with Pythagorean teaching; see A1 (line 28) and 31 DK.

37. See Boyancé, *Le culte de Muses*, pp. 95–103. On the importance of incantations and purifications, see also the conclusion, pp. 350–351.

38. Iambl. *V.P.* 31.196 (ἰατρεύειν τὸ πάθος); cf. 25.110 and Porphyry
V.P. 30: κατεκήλει δὲ ῥυθμοῖς καὶ μέλεσι καὶ ἐπῳδαῖς τὰ ψυχικὰ
πάθη καὶ τὰ σωματικά; see also 32, 33, 35. This may be connected
with the morning and evening purification songs among the
Pythagoreans.
39. Cf. the expressions of Philodemus (*De Mus.* 4 col. 6.13–18,
p. 69 K) about songs of sorrow being able ἰατρεύειν τῆς λύπης. See
also Plutarch *Quaest. Conv.* 657a, about the power of θρηνῳδία to
inspire pity and suppress sorrow.
40. Iambl. *V.P.* 15.64–65.
41. "Aristotele e Aristotelismo nell' estetica antica," *Studi it. fil.
class.* 2 (1922) 1–147; "Un nuovo capitolo della retorica e della
Sofistica," *ibid.*, 148–201.
42. For Empedocles, the tradition is traced to Aristotle (A1 and
19 DK); see also Diogenes Laert. 8.2.58. For Pythagoras, references
are more obscure. They are commented upon by Rostagni in the
articles mentioned above. Empedocles is presented as a disciple of
Pythagoras in Diog. Laert. 8.2.54.
43. The passage in Aristophanes *Birds* 1555, where the verb
applies to Socrates, means the same, as the context shows. Yet irony
makes it a shade more subtle; see n. 47.
44. The context even adds θυσίαις τε καὶ εὐχαῖς καὶ ἐπῳδαῖς
γοητεύοντες.
45. Cf. 271c: ἐπειδὴ λόγου δύναμις τυγχάνει ψυχαγωγία τις.
46. *V.P.* 18.
47. It will also be remembered that Aristophanes applies the notion
to Socrates in *Birds* 1555, in the meaning of summoning the dead,
but with an undeniable hint at deceiving people by speech; once
more, Socrates is presented as one of the sophists.
48. T. Rosenmeyer even connects it with the ontologic difference
between *logos* and reality, which is firmly put forward by Gorgias in
his treatise *On Being*; see "Gorgias, Aeschylus, and *Apate*," *American
Journal of Philology* 76 (1955) 230–232. Though the general skepticism
is of similar quality, the ἀπάτη of rhetoric need not rest on such a
radical basis, and I am not sure that Gorgias felt it did.
49. About such habits in all magic formulas, see J. Combarieu, *La
musique et la magie* (Paris, 1909).
50. See M. H. de Teves Costa, *Euphrosyne* n.s. 2 (1968) 39–57, and
V. Citti, *Il linguaggio religioso nelle tragedie di Eschilo* (Bologna,
1964).
51. The clash of repeated words may be used by Aeschylus in a

less religious context; see *Persians* 1041: δόσιν κακὰν κακῶν κακοῖς, which is very tragic, and yet very like Gorgias. It could even be compared with the passage of the *Palamedes* (B11a36) where Gorgias mentions the scandal for the army of killing Palamedes: εὐεργέτην τῆς Ἑλλάδος Ἕλληνες Ἕλληνα.

52. See also *Od.* 1.62; 5.340 and 423, or Sophocles *Ajax* 430 and 914, Euripides *Trojan Women* 989–990 and *Phoenissae* 636. The mysterious relation will be turned into intellectual suggestions by the sophists and in Plato's *Cratylus*. See also the pun on Thrasymachus' name quoted in Aristotle *Rhet.* 1400b19. On such facts, see P. M. Schuhl, *Essai sur la formation de la pensée grecque* (Paris, 1949), p. 42 and n. 4.

53. See also *Choephori* 949, Δίκα being Διὸς κόρα.

54. This is a more ancient, but more likely, origin than Heraclitus (see p. 234 of Rosenmeyer's article, mentioned above, n. 48).

55. See E. Fraenkel *ad Ag.* 140, and W. Kranz, *Stasimon* (Berlin, 1933), p. 130.

56. *Three Essays*, p. 105.

57. Rostagni, in *Studi it. fil. class.* 2 (1922), pp. 191 ff, traces antithesis and clash of words in the transcription that late authors offer of Pythagoras' speeches, but what he traces is not different from tragedy and cannot provide any safe indication about origin.

58. See also Thrasymachus B1, DK II, p. 326 lines 6 ff (ἡμεῖς δὲ μετὰ μὲν τῶν ἀγαθῶν ἐσωφρονοῦμεν, ἐν δὲ τοῖς κακοῖς ἐμάνημεν) and, for his playing upon words, *Rhet.* 1400b19.

59. 12.53.4: πρῶτος γὰρ ἐχρήσατο τοῖς τῆς λέξεως σχηματισμοῖς περιττοτέροις καὶ τῇ φιλοτεχνίᾳ διαφέρουσιν.

60. This has been suggested by Süss (*Ethos*, p. 84) and accepted by several people. But Pohlenz, Schadewaldt (see *Hellas und Hesperien*, p. 382 n. 5), and Untersteiner (see *I Sofisti*, I, 2nd ed., Milan, 1967, pp. 209–210) share my disbelief. All that can be said is that Gorgias' reference to medicine could offer a starting point for this theory (so Nestle, Rostagni, and others).

61. In order to describe the good action that art and poetry can have on the soul, Aristotle says that people are cured (*Politics* 8.1342a10: ὥσπερ ἰατρείας τυχόντας καὶ καθάρσεως; cf. 1339a–1341b and *Eth. Nic.* 1154b11 ff).

62. This is where I disagree with F. Wehrli's (otherwise quite good) article "Der erhabene und der schlichte Stil in der poetisch-rhetorischen Theorie der Antike," *Phyllobolia Von der Mühll* (Basel, 1946), pp. 9–34.

II. Plato and Conjurers

1. Rostagni, *Studi it. fil. class.* 22 (1922) 155–156, compares this neutrality with the attitude of Antisthenes and with an old Pythagorean saying, quoted by Diog. Laert. 8.32. But this does not imply any influence in any way; what we have is only a plain statement of fact, in each case.

2. See also B3, about the fact that what is, is irreducible to thought or speech.

3. See the different passages quoted p. 7 and note 13. One could add the fact that poetry stirs the part of our soul that is turned toward passion and irritation (*Rep.* 605b); this actual effect of poetry is the very aim and purpose of rhetoric. Thus Plato can speak, shortly afterward, of the ancient opposition between poetry and philosophy (607b).

4. Once more, and in a very surprising way, this criticism is extended to poets, who, in the *Republic*, are described as supporting tyranny (568c).

5. Already in Gorgias, witchcraft was turned into a τέχνη, which means it has become an effort to gather superhuman powers for one's self. The difference is well explained in Philostratus' *Life of Apollonius of Tyana* 1.2.

6. See the cases of Ninus, Theoris, Phryne.

7. See the passage of the *Meno* quoted below, p. 33, where the γόης is taken to prison. There was, of course, a δίκη φαρμάκων for the use of poison. For the contempt of magicians and conjurers in Plato, see *Laws* 649a, quoted below, n. 15, and 909a–d, which is very severe against such practices.

8. "ΓΟΗΣ: zum griechischen Schamanismus," *Rheinisches Museum* 105 (1962) 36–55. The author believes the *polis* to be the cause of such an evolution. It seems difficult to accept this explanation, considering that the change occurs in the fourth century, precisely when the *polis* was in a state of crisis and decay.

9. See Aeschines 3.137, Demosthenes 18.276 and 19.109.

10. The word for "appearing" is φαντάζεσθαι, which suggests phantoms, and it recurs in other similar passages.

11. One should perhaps note that these two "magicians" came from the same western countries as Gorgias. (But their connection with Pythagorean politics, suggested by Rostagni, pp. 178–179, does not seem to me very convincing.)

12. Cf. *Rep.* 556e, where the body στασιάζει αὐτὸ αὑτῷ while the city νοσεῖ.

13. See, in the passage, οὐκ ἔστιν ἄρα τοῦτο, ἀλλὰ φαίνεται; and later, τούτων τῶν φαντασμάτων.

14. 602d: γοητείας οὐδὲν ἀπολείπει.

15. It could be added that in *Laws* 649a, when Plato mentions wine as providing sudden confidence, he says that among the founders of the new city there is no drug to produce fear; God has not given any, nor has one been found out: "for the magicians (γόητας) are not members of our feast." Now rhetoric had boasted it could use words as φάρμακα to produce fear; an allusion to rhetoric is not unlikely here. The hostility to magicians is anyhow made clear.

16. I did not use the fact that, in the beginning of the *Protagoras*, the discovery of the various sophists is a close imitation of Homer's style in the νέκυια; this may be just a nice game of learned allusion. Still, the atmosphere is remarkable.

17. The interpretation in the Budé translation rests on an impossible construction; the translator shrank from the idea that the *logos* could be an ἐπῳδή!

18. See the double meaning of the word in tragedy: the φάρμακον can be a poison (*Medea, Ion* 845, 1221), or a drug producing certain feelings (*Andr.* 157) or making people disappear (*Or.* 1497); it may also have an honest, medical meaning (so *Prom.* 249, 475; Sophocles frs. 514.4, 733; Eur. *Hipp.* 389, 516, 699, fr. 292).

19. Yet, in *Politicus* 280e, the art of antidotes (ἀλεξιφάρμακα) is given as the object of magic (μαγευτικήν).

20. "La pharmacie de Platon," *Tel Quel* 32 (1968) 3–48, and 33 (1968) 18–58. According to him, the magic or poisonous φάρμακον is writing, whereas the medical and profitable φάρμακον, which can be used as antidote, is the *logos*. This is not wholly convincing, and the article does not deal with Plato's actual direct meaning, which is what we are trying to grasp.

21. It has been suggested by F. Dümmler, *Akademika* (Giessen, 1889), p. 22, that the mention of magic in connection with an *epitaphios*, in the beginning of the *Menexenus* (see above, p. 31), was a direct allusion to Gorgias. I doubt very much that the allusion can be so precise, especially since the voice is mentioned and Gorgias could not actually have delivered his *epitaphios*.

22. γραφείς, as opposed to ἀληθείᾳ λεχθείς. The choice of words shows that Gorgias is thinking about written prose, which was to be so important in Isocrates' activity.

23. The relation between rhetoric and medicine is on an utterly

different level from the relation between emotion and physical madness, studied in Flashar's article in *Hermes* 84 (1956) 12–48.

24. This is the very question that Socrates came to ask (447c: βούλομαι γὰρ πυθέσθαι παρ' αὐτοῦ τίς ἡ δύναμις τῆς τέχνης τοῦ ἀνδρός); it is repeated over and over again (see 448e: τίνος Γοργίας ἐπιστήμων, and cf. 449c, 450c).

25. The date of this dialogue places it in the same period as the *Gorgias*, whatever the exact year of the latter's composition.

26. He adds the contrast with gymnastic, which prepares the reader for the description of the real arts, given in 464ff. On this presence of gymnastic, see below, pp. 48 and 56.

III. Rhetoric and the Classification of Arts in the Fourth Century B.C.

1. This is well formulated in Kennedy, *Art of Persuasion*, pp. 17–18: "Plato's criticisms of rhetoric were answered from two directions. Isocrates tried to provide a practical reply. . . . The theoretical refutation of Plato was to come from the friendlier but no less ruthless hand of Aristotle." On the attitude of Plato and Aristotle toward rhetoric, see E. L. Hunt, in *Studies . . . J. A. Winans* (New York, 1925), pp. 3–60.

2. See also 500a–b, 520a–b.

3. This art is here called δικαιοσύνη and in 520b, δικαστική. Some manuscripts offer the reading δικαστικὴ in the three sentences of our passage. This very hesitation in vocabulary shows that the notion, for describing an art, was new; cf. the same hesitation on the name to be given to timocracy, in the *Republic*.

4. See [Plut.] *Ten Orators* 2, and the anonymous *Bios Isocr.* 1.8 ff.

5. His name comes in three times in 270c. On the discussions raised by the attribution of such a notion to Hippocrates, see, for instance, A. Diès, *Autour de Platon*, I (Paris, 1927), pp. 30–45. Plato may very well have added something of his own to the usual description of Hippocrates' rationalistic and scientific ambition. See also P. M. Schuhl, "Platon et la médecine," *Revue des études grecques* 73 (1960) 73–79.

6. To use this repetition as an argument against the authenticity of the *Nicocles* is most unreasonable; in the *Antidosis*, Isocrates repeats, or quotes, from his former works several passages that he thought important.

Notes to Pages 53–61

7. *De Oratore* 1.30ff. The argument is so audacious that Scaevola does not understand it.

8. On this aspect of Isocrates' philosophy, see mainly Eino Mikkola, *Isokrates* (Helsinki, 1954), and the recent thesis (Paris, Nanterre) of J. P. Levet, soon to be published.

9. He only once uses τερθρεία, or charlatanism, against the artificial skill of the sophists (among them Gorgias); this is more severe than Plato, perhaps because Isocrates did not quite see the meaning or bearing of ontological discussion in general.

10. When one sees the subtlety of such polemic, it is impossible not to feel vexed at the harsh simplification of some commentaries, e.g., in the Budé series, the footnote saying: "Le parallèle entre la philosophie et la gymnastique est un lieu commun philosophique: on le retrouve chez Platon (*Gorgias*, 464b) avec des expressions très proches de celles d'Isocrate." All the excitement lies in the difference and distinction between these "expressions très proches."

11. See *Soph.* 12–13 and 14–15; for natural gifts, see *Antidosis* 187–192.

12. His description of the aim of education, in the *Protrepticus*, is polemic against Isocrates. The end of the *Nicomachean Ethics* is open polemic against Isocrates *Antidosis* 80 ff.

13. About the *Gryllus*, see the fine reconstruction by F. Solmsen, *Die Entwicklung der aristotelischen Logik und Rhetorik* (Berlin, 1929), pp. 196–207.

14. On the important difference in conception see below, pp. 62 ff.

15. It is a τέχνη even in the first section of book 1: 1354a7–11 corrects the condemnation of the previous lines. The text says that people practice rhetoric in a way that is no τέχνη, but that this state of things can now be altered and a τέχνη found out.

16. These words are a rash condemnation of all previous τέχναι. Aristotle says that his predecessors have contributed οὐδὲν ὡς εἰπεῖν ... μόριον (1354a12); the text ὀλίγον for οὐδὲν ὡς εἰπεῖν seems to be an attempt to mitigate the condemnation.

17. 1354a13: αἱ γὰρ πίστεις ἔντεχνόν ἐστι μόνον, τὰ δ' ἄλλα προσθῆκαι.

18. 453a: πειθοῦς δημιουργός ἐστιν ἡ ῥητορική.

19. The word is commented upon by Cope-Sandys in a long note (edition of the *Rhetoric*, Cambridge, 1877, ad loc.), which does not mention either Plato or Isocrates. M. Dufour in the introduction to his edition in the Budé series (Paris, 1932), p. 33, says it is Platonic vocabulary, but does not allude to Isocrates. Solmsen, who has an

excellent analysis of the relation between Isocrates and Aristotle, does not mention this particular point.

20. 1355b9: ἡ ῥητορική, ἀλλὰ καθάπερ ἡ διαλεκτική.

21. 1355a14, answering *Phaedrus* 271c ff.

22. Cf. *Ref. Soph.* 183a37–b48, *Top.* 1.1, 100a27 ff.

23. The priority and evolution have been discussed at some length by Rabe, Kantelhardt, Solmsen, and others (see the discussion in Solmsen's book). That the first section is prior to the second is obvious. Whether the first sentence belongs to it could be doubted. But, apart from all other reasons, the two classifications are so different that one does not feel quite happy at the idea of their having been written directly together.

24. Perhaps the connection is suggested by the σοφιστικοῖς λόγοις mentioned in 1359b11; see below, n. 26.

25. For the difference, see Hunt, *Studies . . . J. A. Winans.*

26. We could add 1359b9 ff, where rhetoric combines two sources, knowledge of logical analysis and political knowledge of characters, so that it resembles both dialectic and the speeches of the sophists. But this is practically similar to 1356a, with the bright word "analytic" replacing "dialectic" in the first part of the sentence; on that change, see Solmsen *Aristotelischen Logik und Rhetorik*, p. 225 n. 2. Another classification, by Aelius Aristides, will be mentioned in the next chapter.

27. It is therefore in a very particular and limited application that this simile may be called, with Solmsen, p. 203 n. 1, an "aristotelischen Vergleich."

IV. Logic versus Magic: Aristotle and Later Writers

1. The second development considers what is common to all kinds of speeches. On this structure, see Solmsen *Aristotelischen Logik und Rhetorik*, pp. 223–225.

2. Cf. Kennedy, *Art of Persuasion*, p. 123: "The work is more analytical than instructional."

3. Plutarch also feels uneasy about the importance of such elements; and, characteristically enough, he says that they are part of the ἀπάτη in speech (*De Audiendis Poetis* 41c: ἔχει δέ τι καὶ ἡ λέξις ἀπατηλόν, ὅταν ἡδεῖα καὶ πολλὴ καὶ μετ' ὄγκου τινὸς καὶ κατασκευῆς ἐπιφέρηται τοῖς πράγμασι).

4. Rostagni, in *Studi it. fil. class.* 2 (1922) 91–92, rightly observes that the description exactly suits Menander.

5. On the meaning of this "clarity" and its various applications, see Kennedy, pp. 104–108. Aristotle soon adds another quality of style, namely, that it should be neither mean nor exaggerated. Yet this is nothing more than an addition; and I should not translate, as one generally does (so Cope-Sandys and Dufour), "one of the virtues of style is clarity," but "the virtue of style is clarity" (1404b1: ὡρίσθω λέξεως ἀρετὴ σαφῆ εἶναι). Solmsen must have felt likewise, for he adds (p. 227 n. 3): "die *primäre ἀρετὴ λέξεως*.

6. See also the idea of ἁρμόττειν (1404b13, 1405a10).

7. In the part on τάξις, he is less severe; see 1414b31, 1418a35, 1419b3–4, which are neutral or favorable. There is one criticism in this section, though, bearing on surprise in a too abrupt beginning (1416a3).

8. Even the fact that he left so many important texts without presenting them himself with as much art as possible implies some disregard for the power of style.

9. 1458a18.

10. See G. F. Else's commentary (*Aristotle's Poetics*, Cambridge, Mass., 1957), pp. 567–568.

11. Or, according to Else ad loc., the "costuming."

12. See later 1453b8: ἀτεχνότερον. The contempt is based on the same reasons as Plato's condemnation of rhetoric. It may be added that, in Aristotle's previous sentence, song is counted as the greatest of ἡδυσμάτων, which is quite in line with Platonic criticism. At the end of the *Poetics*, the same idea is repeated, and the change of words is interesting, for ψυχαγωγεῖν is there replaced by δι' ἃς αἱ ἡδοναὶ συνίστανται μάλιστα (1462a16).

13. He afterwards (1408b19–20) says that this style should be used either thus or with irony, as in Gorgias and in Plato's *Phaedrus*: of course, this is but one aspect of Gorgias' tragic diction.

14. Wehrli, in *Phyllobolia Von der Mühll*, p. 27. Rostagni, in *Studi it fil. class.* 2 (1922) 124, adds a similar gap for the μῦθος.

15. Kennedy's *Art of Persuasion in Greece* deals only with Greece and stops at the end of Hellenistic rhetoric; Norden's *Antike Kunstprosa* (Leipzig, 1898) reaches, as the complete title indicates, down to the Renaissance.

16. For a good analysis of his style, see Norden, pp. 131–140. This style, in fact, is compared with Gorgias' style and traced to "the sophists" (pp. 138–139).

17. Cf. Burkert in *Rheinisches Museum* 105 (1962) 36–55.

18. Cf. *Life of Apollonius of Tyana* 7.39, end; Philostratus says he

will not insist, since the practice is condemned both φύσει . . . καὶ νόμῳ.

19. Calling the help of a magician is to use σοφίσμασι (p. 294 Loeb); this is in keeping with what we saw in Plato. Magicians are called ψευδοσόφους (p. 298 Loeb). Later we again find τοῖς σοφισταῖς τούτοις.

20. Philostratus *V.S.*, pp. 523, 590; see Bowersock, *Greek Sophists in the Roman Empire* (Oxford, 1969), pp. 116–117.

21. Bowersock, p. 70. See also his remarks about the ἰατροσοφιστής, pp. 19 and 67, and about the importance of dreams in medicine, pp. 73–74.

22. The word used for them is κορυβαντιῶσιν; it is critical but all the same reveals the new tone and sends us back to what Plato used to blame.

23. Apart from the passage in 8.4, see 13.2, where he explains that orators can be inspired by their predecessors, just as the Delphic priestess was inspired by the god. When they read beautiful passages, the authors receive "emanations," which carry them away; and even those who are not of an inspired nature are then "caught in the others' enthusiasm" (συνενθουσιῶσιν).

24. Whether such a τέχνη exists, he feels, is a problem (2.1: εἰ ἔστιν ὕψους τις ἢ βάθους τέχνη); and he often points out that a natural gift is the main thing. Yet he admits that τέχνη is useful and starts with this idea (2.2–3).

25. Both are mentioned in 37, where he uses the catchword ἀντίστροφος; in 43, we again find the comparison with medicine; see also 2.93.

26. 54: τοῦτ' ἐν τῇ ψυχῇ καὶ τοῖς τῶν πόλεων πράγμασι ῥητορικὴ φαίνεται. Isocrates would have enjoyed the addition of political life.

27. This does not mean that the notion of "magic" is being restored; it was never to be. Our author uses ψυχαγωγεῖν in the low meaning of pleasing the audience, instead of opening its mind; and γόητα is synonymous with ἀλαζόνα in 49.367.

28. Κατὰ τῶν ἐξορχουμένων, p. 412.

29. Aristides, like Gorgias, refused to see a major difference between prose and poetry (45.4–13 Keil); but this did not imply an attempt to make prose become poetical. Poets invented poetry χάριτός τινος ἕνεκα καὶ ψυχαγωγίας, but works in prose are more useful.

30. *Greek Sophists in the Roman Empire*, p. 58.

31. On the importance of these cities, see *ibid.*, chap. 2: "Cities of the Sophists."

32. P. 221, §519: ὡμίλει δὲ σοφιστῶν μάλιστα Γοργίᾳ τῷ Λεοντίνῳ.

33. P. 257, §590: he mentions, together, the influence of tragedy and of "the ancient sophists."

34. P. 263, §604.

35. See the above reference and p. 213, §501, or p. 209, §493. The word is used in other works of Philostratus. The importance of Gorgias for the second sophistic is very well presented by Norden, pp. 379–386, where more references can be found.

36. See above, n. 33.

37. P. 271, §620.

38. For the metaphors of song and the insistence on rhythm, see the numerous quotations collected by Norden, pp. 377–379.

39. For the speaker compared with the Sirens, see also Themistius *Or.* 28.341c.

40. See also θέλγειν used for the influence of speech, p. 208, §491, and the same word combined with the reference to Orpheus and Thamyris, in the case of the ancient sophists, in Philostratus' letters (p. 364).

41. See, for Nicetes, ὑπόβακχος δὲ καὶ διθυραμβώδης (p. 217, §511); for Scopelian, διθυραμβώδη (p. 218, §514); for Polemo, θερμὴ καὶ ἐναγώνιος (p. 232, §542).

42. Letter to P. Dennery, *Nouvelle revue française*, June 1912.

43. This form of inspiration may be connected with the similar value attributed by Freud to the unconscious self; but the interest of Breton was not psychological or turned toward psychoanalysis. On the question, see the study by Starobinsky mentioned below, n. 45.

44. In "Entrée des mediums."

45. J. Starobinsky, "Freud, Breton, Myers," in *André Breton: Essais recueillis par M. Ergeldinger* (Neuchâtel, 1970), p. 171.

46. In "L'amour fou."

47. That is why one generally does not know who is speaking in this kind of novel; see R. Barthes, *S/Z* (Paris, 1970), pp. 48–49.

48. Such a trend of thought already appears in some remarks of authors like Nietzsche and Valéry. A good example of the general doctrine can be found in T. Todorov, *Théorie de la littérature* (Paris, 1965). Among its main representatives are V. Chlovski, R. Jakobson, and V. Propp, whose names should be mentioned here, together with that of G. Genette (*Figures*, Paris, 1966, 1969, 1972).

49. See *S/Z*, pp. 26, 153, 172.

Index

Index

Index